PIAF AND CERDAN

PIAF AND CERDAN

A Hymn to Love

Dominique Grimault and Patrick Mahé

Translated from French by Barbara Mitchell

W.H. ALLEN · LONDON

COMET

Copyright © Editions Robert Laffont, SA., Paris 1983
English translation copyright © W. H. Allen & Co. PLC 1984

First published in France by Editions Robert Laffont 1983
First British edition 1984

Phototypeset by Input Typesetting Ltd, London
Printed and bound in Great Britain by
Biddles Ltd, Guildford & King's Lynn,
for the publishers W. H. Allen & Co. PLC,
44 Hill Street, London W1X 8LB

ISBN 0 491 03362 1 (W. H. Allen hardcover edition)
ISBN 0 86379 032 1 (Comet Books softcover edition)

Contents

'He died in the heavens so I know he's there'

Edith Piaf

1

The Paris–New York Plane Crash

At 3.55 Paris time on the night of 27–8 October 1949 the alarm was raised in Santa Maria, the main island in the Azores. There was a mad scramble to get a rescue operation together. Eight planes took off. Two Portuguese Navy patrol boats put to sea. Then silence returned, heavy with anxiety. Radios, telephones, teleprinters were all poised for the news that didn't come.

Finally, Air France issued a first communiqué expressing concern. But no one could believe there had been an accident. There had never been any accidents on the Paris–New York route. How could the plane have disappeared? The atmosphere at Orly was tense: the pilots congregated and the flight engineers talked amongst themselves. Monsieur Daurat, the old chief pilot who had been friendly with Mermoz, the founder of the first intercontinental airline, put a brave face on it but there were tears in his eyes.

Friday looked like being one long ordeal. Flights landed and took off as usual but the minutes ticked by slowly and heavily as the tragedy unfolded.

12.25: amidst growing concern, an Air France Constellation FBA-ZL took off for the Azores with a team of investigators led by M. de Levis-Mirepoix, chief pilot Boulet and a six-man crew. It was to land at Santa Maria at 4.40 p.m.

3.00 p.m: the FBA-ZL search plane requested permission to land directly on Sao Miguel Island, on the Santa Ana airfield, eighty miles from Santa Maria.

'Hurry up, Loulou. We're going to be late.'

'Just a minute. I want to buy a few rolls of film.'

It was nine o'clock on a cold grey morning in New York. Loulou Barrier, Edith Piaf's manager, unconsciously tightened his scarf as he crossed Lexington Avenue. He rushed into the first drugstore he came across. Marc Bonel, the accordionist, waited for him in the doorway and stopped the next taxi.

Barrier rummaged through his pockets and pulled out a few dollars. All around him people were talking excitedly. He kept hearing the words 'Paris. . .Air France. . .Cerdan. . .New York'. The words rang through his head. He asked the salesman: 'What's going on? What's happened? What are you all talking about?'

The man's reaction was slightly disturbing. He stared at Barrier somewhat warily. 'Haven't you heard?'

'About what?'

'The Paris–New York plane has disappeared. It's been on the radio all morning.'

3.55 p.m. Paris time: the first telegram arrived from Sao Miguel. It was terse and its message terrible: 'FBA-ZN found on fire on Algarvia peak, north-east of Sao Miguel. Stop. Search plane 6250 reports survivors. Stop. I am going there immediately.'

As the taxi sped across Queensboro Bridge on the way to La Guardia airport, Loulou Barrier and Marc Bonel stared at the road ahead. Edith's excited voice was still ringing in their ears. 'I'm counting on you folks tomorrow morning. I've told Marcel you'll be there.' It was always

8

the same. Edith had never been able to get up in the morning. She had every excuse, of course: for the last two weeks she had been giving two performances an evening in the Versailles, the smart Broadway night-club. She went to bed late and got up late. Anyway, long-distance flights were not yet in the habit of arriving on time.

On Northern Boulevard in Queens the traffic was moving fairly freely. Marc Bonel consulted his watch. Marcel's plane was due in at 9.30. Marc was supposed to be filming his arrival in a quarter of an hour's time.

People were still keeping their fingers crossed at Orly. But the airline pilots had doubts as soon as they looked at the map. 'The reconnaissance plane could have been wrong. Peasants and shepherds who rushed to the scene would have been taken for survivors . . .'

Santa Ana is two-and-a-half-hours' walk or mule ride from the place where the plane came down. The Air France chief at the refuelling base made his way through the mountains with a search party. Time passed more and more slowly.

Back in Paris, Daurat and the man in charge of operations also pored over a map of the Azores. The Orly Transmission Service was on the alert. The map of Sao Miguel was studied frenziedly. There it was, the Rodonta peak, 3,500 feet high. The plane must have crashed into the peak at 260 miles per hour – four miles a minute. At that speed, given the Constellation's weight of 46 tonnes, the passengers would have died instantaneously.

Hope diminished by the hour. But all that mattered was to try and carry out any possible rescue work. No one dared be more specific. Fire had obviously broken out on board but only after the crash, so anyone who had survived would have had time to get away. But an accident was inconceivable with Radio Range, the radar

9

system which automatically guided the pilot to his destination. Perhaps the altimeter had gone wrong.

6.30 p.m: a statement was issued from Santa Maria: 'The search party is making headway but is encountering rain and fog.' Transatlantic flights from Paris to New York were diverted via Iceland.

In her flat at 136 East 67th Street and Lexington, Edith slept on. Her friend Genevieve, wife of the journalist Felix Lévitan, had risen quite early, and in all innocence telephoned the Air France counter at La Guardia to find out what time the Paris–New York flight would be arriving. There was a panic-stricken voice at the other end. The employee was in such a state that she blurted out the news about the catastrophe without a thought for Genevieve's feelings. Genevieve was distraught. She ran to her room and shut herself in. When she returned to the sitting-room, still numb, the television flashed out its first cruel message: 'It is doubtful that there are any survivors . . .'

Orly 7.00 p.m.: The search party reported that the FBA-ZN plane had burned from 4.00 in the morning to 2.00 p.m. The plane was in ashes. This time there was no room for doubt. It was a terrible catastrophe. There were no survivors. The Azores had lived up to their meaning in Portuguese – 'vultures'.

In the airport, the staff kept their eyes down as though paralysed. Daurat, the old head, shrank still further into his seat. He forgot to light the cigarette that was always in his hand. Drained of all emotion and surrounded by his team, he faced the press. Choosing his words carefully, he said: 'Gentlemen, this news causes us immense distress . . .'

10

Loulou Barrier and Marc Bonel spent nearly four hours at La Guardia praying for a miracle. They brought back with them to Edith's flat the full weight of the brutal tragedy. It was 1.30 p.m. Robert Chauvigny, the pianist who accompanied Edith so well and was a professional to the tips of his fingers, had arrived in the meantime with the grief-stricken look of someone who already knew the worst.

Edith's little world stood united. Everyone was immured in their own silent grief. All eyes were on the door at the end of the corridor which, sooner or later, was going to open. She would emerge. Who was going to tell her? Instinctively, everyone looked at Genevieve Lévitan. Genevieve had been one of the connecting links between Edith and Marcel. Her husband had always been the champion's number one confidant. Genevieve and Edith were now inseparable. But Genevieve's expression said 'No'.

'Why didn't you wake me?'

Edith's voice was the last thing any of them wanted to hear. She was wearing a dressing-gown and was still half asleep, her hair hardly combed. No one dared reply.

'And where's Marcel?'

She thought they were playing a joke on her. She looked behind the door. Her expression and intonation changed. She was ready to get into the spirit of what she took for a game.

'Marcel, stop it, please. Why are you hiding?'

She glanced round the sitting-room. You could have cut the atmosphere with a knife. Genevieve turned her head away helplessly. Chauvigny and Bonel didn't know where to look.

Then Edith grew irritated. 'What's going on? What's happening? Where's Marcel? Didn't he leave? Is he still in Paris? Tell me, damn it!'

Barrier realised he had to say something. He took Edith gently by the shoulders and whispered: 'Dearest Edith, be brave. Something's happened to Marcel.'

Edith's voice broke: 'What, Loulou? What are you telling me . . . what?'

2

The Clash in Madison Square Garden

Marcel was over thirty when he first went to the United States. For a boxer like him, who had already put everything he had into the sport, that was quite old. He was about to take on his one hundred-and-eighth fight. He began aged seventeen in Casablanca and had already spent thirteen years in the ring. He had won all the titles in Europe. He had taken quite a few knocks but his knees had never touched the canvas. Cerdan had always remained on his feet. And, until now, he had never been defeated, although he had been disqualified twice, in 1939 in London when he faced Craster, and in 1942 in Algiers against Buttin.

If it had not been for the war, the US would certainly have discovered him in 1939, after he won the title of European champion in a fight against the Italian Turiello. The war shattered his dreams. He was left to champ at the bit and go on with his training. But once that wretched interlude was over Cerdan was off, leaving behind the country which set such store by his fists.

Madison Square Garden, New York, 6 December 1946
The crowd grew quiet and stared at him. People must have thought this foreigner rather strange. Silent and impassive, he was lost in concentration. It was as though his features were frozen in a steely mask. He had a fixed

scowl on his face. He sat on his stool in the corner, looking pale in his sky-blue robe. His manager, Lucien Roupp, leaned over him and insisted on talking to him. He was trying to arouse his interest in something – in the weather, the people in the hall, anything. He mentioned the name of Harry Marcson, the first American to have faith in Cerdan. He was the head of the Madison Square Garden press service. He had praised the 'Frenchie' to all the New York journalists, who would now have a chance to judge him for themselves. It was no good. Cerdan remained impassive. Roupp could not even get him to turn his head ten degrees. Cerdan was oblivious to everything except his opponent sitting on the other side of the ring, Georgie Abrams.

But the fight had not yet begun. Harry Baloogh, the Madison's official Master of Ceremonies was speaking. Bald, with a crumpled face, and too thin for his off-the-peg dinner-jacket, he droned into the microphone in his New York accent: 'Ladies and gentlemen, please . . . in this corner . . . Mar-cel Cer-dan!'

The last people in the ring moved off, leaving the two boxers and the referee, the bald Mr Ruby Goldstein in short-sleeved white shirt and black bow-tie. Abrams and Cerdan had turned their backs on each other as if they didn't know the other was there or wanted to avoid seeing each other. All of a sudden, as the referee opened the fight, they turned round and walked towards each other. Cerdan's face remained serious but the movement unleashed all the strength he was holding back, all the pent-up muscle power and nervous energy. Cerdan's eyes bored into Abrams' to guess, sense and forestall his moves. A fierce battle began – one which was to last ten rounds.

Georgie Abrams had the face and guts of a boxer who has given and taken a good many knocks. Since the beginning of 1946 his position had wavered between third and eighth amongst the US middleweights. This former marine had won few victories in knock-outs. George was a battler rather than a hard hitter. When he boxed Tony Zale (later to become world champion) in 1941, Georgie survived fifteen rounds with a fractured rib and one eye closed – some people thought it would be closed for good. To cut a long story short, Abrams was a moral and physical bull of a man.

Cerdan, deep in concentration, tense and pale, immediately realised what kind of an opponent the Americans had selected for him. But this did not scare him. You had to do what you had to do! Besides, Abrams brought back good wartime memories. When the Americans landed in Algiers he had beaten up endless numbers of Yankees in the infamous Allied contests where you exchanged a ration of blows for a carton of cigarettes. But there was a world of difference between those soldiers' dogfights and the clash that was to take place that evening at Madison Square Garden in New York.

Shortly before Marcel's departure for New York the French newspaper *Miroir-Sprint* had organised a gala dinner. Marcel was flanked by Thil, Pladner, Routis, Holtzer, Angelman, Criqui and Tenet – seven former French world champions. Georges Carpentier, a 'gentleman of the ring' who had fought in every boxing division, was also there.

Carpentier rose to his feet during the meal and made an impromptu speech. He told Cerdan: 'In a few days, Marcel, you will be landing in a country where everything will amaze you. You will see buildings which reach up to the sky. You will be met by dozens of journalists who will inundate you with questions. You will respond politely to these people, who you don't know, and they will like

15

you. Beneath what can be rough exteriors, Americans are basically wonderful people. It's up to you to put across the very special attributes of the French boxer. Because, Marcel, there are some traits which are almost exclusively French. We can fight and we have guts. We've got everything it takes. Now you just go out there and make sure you come back world champion.'

Marcel embarked on the *Ile de France* at Cherbourg with Lucien Roupp, his manager, a leading boxing expert, and Jo Longman, his adviser. The boat had nothing in common with the opulent liners of the pre-war period. It had been requisitioned by the British and had served as a troop-carrier. Instead of saloons and dining-rooms there were dormitories everywhere. Marcel had had no idea conditions on board would be so bad. The passengers were crammed together. He had been given preferential treatment – and what treatment! – with a fifteen-by-twelve-foot cabin with two beds, a bedside table, a chest of drawers, four armchairs, and a connecting bathroom. A steward had whispered in his ear: 'You're in luck. This is a general's cabin.'

The crossing lasted eight days. The weather was stormy and the only sunshine they had was provided by the popular actress Simone Simon. Cerdan played draughts with her every afternoon and enjoyed winning. In the end Simone Simon flashed him a mischievous smile and said 'I'm not very good at *dames* (French for draughts); I was better in the *Lac aux Dames* (the title of one of her films).' Marcel, who hadn't grasped the allusion, smiled politely.

The two of them were involved in an event which was the talking-point of the crossing. A young female stowaway gave birth to a little girl on board. Henry Torrès, a star of the Paris bar, decided to start a collection for the impoverished mother. Simone Simon and Marcel Cerdan approached the passengers for contributions. A tidy 120,000 francs was raised.

The next day a Parisian journalist put his own interpretation on the story under front-page banner headlines that read 'SIMONE SIMON AND MARCEL CERDAN HAVE A CHILD ON THE ILE DE FRANCE'. It made a good story.

The weather was beautiful when they arrived. As Carpentier had predicted, Marcel was taken aback by New York. Several people were waiting for him on the quay. There was Lew Burston, the boxing agent who liaised between Europe and the US; Sammy Ritchmann, the manager; Nate Rogers, the Twentieth-Century Sporting Club promoter; and Robert Bré, a correspondent attached to various French newspapers. The welcome they gave him was an indication of how important his visit was felt to be.

Also there to welcome him was Jo Rizzo, who had previously got on the wrong side of the French police but had later settled down in the US and become a good citizen. He was to be Cerdan's chauffeur. Cerdan moved into the Shelton Hotel on Lexington Avenue, a stone's throw from Madison Square Garden and Broadway, places with a magical ring to their names. Lew Burston invited him to lunch at Toots Shore, the New York equivalent of Fouquet's. Burston, a First World War veteran, had spent the next twenty years in Paris, where he had been a familiar figure on the sporting scene. He had an eye for all the good boxers, and he had always given the New York public their money's worth. Before Cerdan there had been Peter Sanstol, the Norwegian, nicknamed 'Fireball' by the Americans; the Belgian René Devos 'the Red Devil'; and Pedro Montanez, a fighter famous for his showmanship.

In the evening, Burston took Marcel, Roupp and

Longman to dinner at the Bistro, a French restaurant on Third Avenue decorated in rococo style with white table-cloths adorned with a single rose. But Marcel's first official visit was to the Twentieth-Century Club, the museum of the journalist-cum-collector Nat Fleisher in Madison Square Garden, a sort of academy of world boxing. Marcel was both intrigued and disturbed by his visit. The first photo to catch his eye when he went into a large room, 36 feet by 18, was that of Georgie Abrams. Just from his forceful portrait in this hall of fame Cerdan realised it was going to be a tough fight. He was then presented with the poster for the contest – it was the first time he had headed an American bill – and Abrams' was the only face on it. The poster was in red, yellow and black.

Mike Jacobs himself had insisted on being there that evening. The ageing man, whose name was synonymous with boxing in Madison Square Garden, was very ill. But he had put off a vacation in Florida for Cerdan. It was a good sign.

Jacobs and Cerdan got on well.

'I hope you'll stay with us a long time. We'll work well together.'

Marcel was very flattered by these words of welcome. But he felt much less positive when he visited the Stillman Gymnasium, famous throughout the world as having served as a springboard for the best US boxers. He didn't dare say so to the people round him but he started to feel ill at ease almost as soon as he set foot in this boxing factory on Eighth Avenue which stank of cheap cigars and shady deals. He preferred the calm and cleanliness of a more modest hall at the Catholic Youth Organisation on the first floor of a building on 11th Street. Boxer by day, by night Marcel became a tourist. The smallest thing entertained him: the permanently revolving doors of the Shelton Hotel; the lift light which was always red (indicating the lifts were perpetually busy); the Empire State Building, which he visited with the jazz guitarist Django Reinhardt. And of course, and above all, the cinema.

A poster for the Paramount Cinema on Broadway caught his eye. They were showing *Blue Skies* with Bing Crosby and Fred Astaire. When he went into the cinema with Jo and Lucien the film had been on for three-quarters of an hour. But that didn't put Marcel off. He made his companions sit through not only the rest of the film, the news, the documentary, three musical attractions – Stan Kenton and his orchestra, Dean Murphy and the King Cole Trio – but also the main feature again, from start to finish. They were in there for four hours.

Everything was going very well – too well.

One morning when he woke up, Marcel complained of violent pains in his back. Roupp decided to call a doctor. 'Nothing serious' was the doctor's diagnosis. 'Your boxer has caught a chill. He's suffering from stiffness.' The treatment consisted of prolonged deep massage. Needless to say, training was not to be pushed.

After this incident, Cerdan and Roupp, feeling oppressed and beset by journalists, decided to leave town. Jo Rizzo drove them to Flushing, at the near end of Long Island, forty minutes away by car. They were put up by Luis Indaco in a homely atmosphere. It was easy to organise a routine there: jogging in the morning, gymnastics in the afternoon, then some light fist-work. As the pain eased, Marcel started putting his heart into it. He was sparring with a young black, Jerome Richardson, when there was another incident. Richardson rolled his shoulders, dreaming that he was fighting in the world championship and stupidly threw a hard jab at Cerdan's right eye. At the end of the training session Marcel was almost blind in that eye. He was forced to rest for three days. But Richardson had his comeuppance. When

Cerdan got back in the ring, the insolent young man found he was being approached by a different boxer. A few one-twos and Richardson was doubled up in pain. Marcel had hit him in the stomach, without holding back. Richardson suffered so badly that he threw his arms out at Marcel in despair as though to say 'Are you crazy? You're really hurting me!'

Cerdan produced a faint smile. 'Well, have you seen my eye?'

Richardson got the message. The next day, having decided to sacrifice his pride, he returned to face Cerdan wearing a stomach-protecter.

Richardson commented: 'I feel sorry for whoever has to fight Cerdan, whether it's Abrams, Graziano or Tony Zale.'

In the Madison Square Garden arena, which was filled with the smoke of innumerable Camels, the only thing you could make out was the dazzling whiteness of the ring in the intense light of a hundred-odd floodlights. Otherwise everything was plunged in darkness, including the 16,971 spectators, the only visible sign of whom was their glowing cigarettes. They had paid a total of $83,859 for this. In the two balcony tiers people were passing round bottles of beer and soda, or sharing peanuts and hot dogs bought from the vendors walking up and down the aisles.

There were shouts and whistles, and people cheered and booed – it sounded like a Gershwin symphony written for Duke Ellington! There was even a chorus of black voices; these were the young blacks from Harlem who dreamed of following in Joe Louis's footsteps. They couldn't afford to buy a coffee, and saved themselves the subway fare, but they always had their dollar entrance fee for the fights. They were not going to miss a single punch.

At the end of the first round, the whole crowd was shouting 'What a fight!' Marcel had won over both the American spectators and the critics who had seen plenty of other good fights and didn't miss a thing. No one was surprised that Abrams should throw himself so ferociously into the match. But what delighted the crowd was that Cerdan gave as good as he got and tried to put one on his opponent as early in the fight as possible. It all went to prove that Mike Jacobs had not been mistaken. But the people who were happiest about this action-packed start to the bout were those in Marcel's corner: Lucien Roupp, Jo Longman, Lew Burston, Jo Rizzo.

It was a tough fight. Lucien Roupp could see from the outset that Cerdan was acting impetuously. 'Calm down Marcel . . . calm down. Get your breath . . . It's going to be a long fight . . . Save yourself,' he kept repeating. He was wasting his time.

At the end of the second round, Marcel's left hook flashed out. It was like lightning. Abrams had no time to fend off the blow. His left eyebrow split open. Marcel continued to hit him. He couldn't be held back. Then he started to tire. Burston cast a slightly worried glance at Longman. Roupp started shouting to him again: 'Calm down, calm down.' Marcel didn't hear: he seemed to be shutting himself off.

Fourth round: Cerdan was stopped by the referee, Ruby Goldstein, who broke up the fight and gave Cerdan a warning for hitting below the belt. The caution was justified but Cerdan's mistake was not unreasonable. Not only had Abrams pulled the belt of his shorts very high but Cerdan's reach was shorter, forcing him to fight close in.

The only worrying thing at this point in the match was

Cerdan's shortness of breath. Roupp feared that he had started off too fast. There were clear signs of it. In the fifth round, Marcel got rid of his gum shield and kicked it high over the ring. He was short of oxygen and had no sense of how much time had gone by and how much was left. He seemed very weary at the end of the fifth round when he returned to his corner. He also seemed to be in a hurry to finish the match. Roupp leaned towards him and pulled his belt. Drenched in sweat, Cerdan's chest heaved up and down. The break between rounds can never provide more than fleeting respite. Depending on how the boxer views the fight, it can seem two seconds long – or an hour.

Cerdan had his eyes fixed on the illuminated panel showing the number of rounds. The number 6 was showing and he thought that this meant the seventh round was about to begin. He had forgotten that in Madison Square Garden the screen indicates the number of the round which is about to begin and not of the one which has just finished. Roupp dared not tell him the truth.

The audience roared with pleasure. Extricating himself from a clinch, Abrams saw an opening. He struck out sharply. Cerdan was rooted to the centre of the ring. He wavered for two seconds. Roupp called out: 'On your guard, Marcel, your guard.'

Marcel didn't take anything in but reacted mechanically, and instinctively raised his gloves. His left eyebrow had opened and blood was trickling down his cheek. The fight had turned into a street brawl. Lew Burston panicked. He thought for a second and shouted out to Longman and Roupp: 'How can we stop the blood?'

Roupp was crouching at the bottom of the steps, his eyes creased up behind his tortoiseshell glasses, the corner of his mouth turned up in a grimace. He did not reply. Blood could always be stopped. What bothered him was Abrams' brutal, flailing advance on his man. Behind him the crowd was suddenly getting excited as though the American spectators sensed the 'Frenchie' was in trouble. In the cheaper seats people were shouting 'Kill him!', 'Kill the frog!', 'Sock him!'

The bell went. This time the rest period came as a deliverance. Longman and Burston were on Cerdan's left, administering emergency first-aid. Burston applied a miraculous product to the smashed eyebrow, temporarily halting the bleeding. On his right was Lucien Roupp: 'Breathe, Marcel, breathe.'

The seventh round was a stalemate: neither boxer managed to gain an advantage. It was blow for blow. There was nothing to choose between Adams and Cerdan in terms of energy, bravery, ferocity and ability to take a lot of beating and then recover.

The eighth round was the hardest for Cerdan. Abrams, who stood rooted like an oak to the middle of the ring, absolutely immovable, subjected him to a barrage of blows. Cerdan circled Abrams, attacking again and again, but he was blocked every time. And now his right eye too was cut.

At the beginning of the ninth round Abrams got over-confident. He thought he had Cerdan under control, but Cerdan was following Roupp's orders to the letter: he held off his attack, went on the defensive and gathered his strength while seeking a way to get back into the fight. Abrams was convinced that he now had Cerdan at his mercy. He misinterpreted his opponent's calculated move as weakness. And that was how Georgie found himself on all fours for the first time in his career.

There was one round left to go. Whatever happened now, Marcel had pulled off a match worthy of a great champion. He had fought American style. In Madison

Square Garden. Against Georgie Abrams. And it was a fight that would be remembered.

Roupp urged Marcel on by reminding him, one by one, of all the things which were dearest to his heart and meant most to him. When Marcel came back to his corner for the last time, he was only three minutes away from glory. Three minutes seems like nothing, but his whole career hung on it and he wouldn't get another chance.

'Marcel, think of them. You've got to win for them.'

Dead with exhaustion, Marcel looked blankly at Roupp. He just couldn't get his breath back. He may not have heard the audience shouting. So Roupp had to go on: 'Marcel, I beg you, for their sake. For Marinette, your wife, and your sons. They're listening to the fight on the radio in Casa. You owe it to them, Marcel, and you know it.'

Roupp had never used this kind of argument before. It wasn't his style. But this was the first time Cerdan had ever given him an opportunity to appeal to his emotions. It was as though Roupp was laying down a card which up till now he had refused to play.

And Cerdan kept on going to the end. He was still fighting when the bell rang. The referee Ruby Goldstein had to lead him back into his corner. He had won. There was no question about it. The referee awarded six rounds to Cerdan, two to Abrams and two tied. The two judges, Frank Forbes and Marty Monrol, gave Marcel a clear lead on points.

His brain was buzzing. He allowed himself to be led into the middle of the ring. Lucien Roupp put his left arm under his right armpit. The photographers set about their business: 'Smile, Marcel, smile, please.' And Marcel smiled mechanically, a professional through and through. Never before had a victory cost him so much physical damage.

The people at the ringside were euphoric. The applause went on and on. People were comparing the Frenchie to the Eiffel Tower and saying that Georgie had fought the best match of his career – and that was undoubtedly the best compliment you could pay Cerdan. Amongst the most enthusiastic were Frank Sinatra and Breda Frazier, considered to be the most beautiful girl in America, who had bet on Abrams but applauded Cerdan's victory out of a sense of fair play. But her husband, John Kelly, the film-maker, was clapping even louder, since he had bet heavily on Marcel. And there were two French people in the first row: Jean Sablon, who was playing on Broadway, and Simone Simon, who was only too delighted to come and cheer her travelling companion.

It was four o'clock in the morning in Paris. But in the Club des Cinq, a fashionable night-spot in Montmartre, they were living on Madison Square Garden time.

The evening had been dedicated to Marcel Cerdan. Everyone was waiting for the good news that was finally announced by Georges Briquet, the star radio and TV presenter. Every Sunday his inexhaustible flow of cheery wit and colourful gossip kept his ten million listeners happy. Briquet, with his smooth round face and chubby build, had become Cerdan's number one fan. He grabbed the microphone, stopped the music, separated the couples and managed to obtain complete silence. He had the knack of getting to people's emotions using very simple words put together so well they made a fitting tribute to a hero's achievement. That evening Marcel was his hero, and he used one superlative after another. Marcel had been extraordinary, marvellous, outstanding, superb, etc., etc.

Briquet glanced round the exclusive gathering. They had all been screened at the entrance. Cerdan's friends and devotees had passed the word round, and gathered like brothers to share the excitement of Marcel's American challenge. Most of them, and particularly the boxers, looked quite unlike their usual selves. There was Marcel Thil, Laurent Dauthuille, Assane Diouf and even Edouard Tenet, all dressed up in pin-striped suits, white shirts and pocket handkerchiefs. They were all smiles, having hung up their boxing gloves for the occasion.

In the midst of the general euphoria Briquet asked Marcel Thil, the former heavyweight champion, for his comments. Thil, the expert, didn't need to be asked twice. Playful, with expansive gestures, he was highly complimentary: 'It was a foregone conclusion.'

In the changing-room, Marcel collapsed in Jo Rizzo's arms. He recovered, but only very slowly. Before leaving Madison Square Garden he had to go to the treatment room. Abrams, showing what a nice guy he was, went with him. Vincent Nardiello, the doctor who sewed four stitches in Marcel's left eyebrow, was solicitous and clapped the victor on the shoulder.

Then the telegrams started flooding in. There was one from Edith Piaf: 'Well done, I was sure you'd make it.' Twenty-four hours earlier Piaf had cabled: 'I shan't be able to sleep a wink. Stop. Remember the whole of Paris is with you. Stop. And little Piaf sends you a piece of her heart.'

3

Meeting in the Club des Cinq

'A child of the streets, Piaf was a sort of reincarnation of the *Mystères de Paris*. She was like one of Hugo's heroines; she had no family and grew up as best she could. She was like a cricket whose songs expressed a poetic, innocent vision of Paris. Paris was her universe. That was where she learned to pass a hat round for her father, and where she found love. True to the ballads, she was unhappy in love, and she sang about her affairs to exorcise her unhappiness. For Piaf had first-hand experience of the painful storybook world of her songs; her voice was the voice of everyone who ever knew its joys and its sorrows. She was the greatest popular singer of our time in the true sense that the songs she sang were of and for the people.'

Tributes to Piaf

You entered an internal courtyard, went down a few steps and came upon a commissionaire complete with cap and gold buttons. The door led into a vast room with a small stage, boxes on all sides, pedestal tables and dark red curtains. The place was invariably packed; all the beautiful people came here to jive. This was the Club des Cinq.

When Michel Emer gave the signal to his orchestra the noise would surge, reach a crescendo, and take off, drowning everything. You couldn't hear yourself speak.

The orchestra was made up of two trumpets, a trombone, a clarinette, four saxes, percussion, a piano, an acoustic guitar and a bass guitar. Emer used his baton like a rod of iron. Sometimes the music was just too loud. People would try to get Emer to keep the volume down. They would ask him if he couldn't possibly make it a bit quieter. He would nod but only proceed to get the brass section going even more strongly. From nine o'clock onwards people danced as though there were no tomorrow. It was just after the war; there was rationing and memories of German uniforms were all too vivid in people's minds. Count Basie's music made your head spin. That was the idea. Michael Emer's favourite piece was 'In the mood'. He had created the atmosphere in the Club des Cinq by using American musical arrangements sent over by his friend Bernstein in New York. The latest was Frances Ash's 'I'm gonna love that guy', which Roy Ventura and Jacques Helian already had their eyes on. Bernstein was in the boxing world over there and worked closely with Jo Longman. With his dark glasses hiding eyes burned by the African sun, Longman symbolised the legend of the Club des Cinq. The five in question were: Captain Lecole, Lieutenant Blenes, Germain Libine, Charly Mittel and Jo. All five had been volunteers in the Second Armoured Division.

Longman's experience was typical of that of the rest of the group. Born in England, when war broke out Longman went to the recruitment bureau in Paris to join up. It was suggested that he should go back to London. In the end he managed to join the Leclerc Army. Enlisted in Algeria and made the sports officer in charge of boxing, it was inevitable that he would meet up with Marcel Cerdan.

They met in Casablanca during a fund-raising gala for Resistance fighters. The match took place in the rain.

Cerdan's opponent was called Milano, and it took Cerdan less than six minutes to polish him off. Despite his disappointment, the loser's manager made a point of shaking Cerdan's hand. The manager was Jo Longman and the date was 31 October 1943. Longman was never in any doubt that he would meet up with Cerdan again after the war – provided there was an afterwards.

At that time people lived a day at a time, and each day that went by brought the five of them closer to fulfilling the pledge they had made to each other: Longman, Lecole, Blenes, Libine and Mittel had sworn to meet up again at the end of the road. And, who knows, perhaps they would make their fortunes together. This was the start of the Club des Cinq.

They took over an enormous cellar in Montmartre, right opposite the newspaper *L'Equipe*. It had belonged to Jean Luchaire, a well-known collaborator, who had been shot in the Fort de Chatillon, with a cigarette hanging from his lips. In the euphoria of the Liberation, the Club des Cinq soon became a fashionable spot. It was a smart place in which to be seen. It was a good place in which to perform. Jean Sablon and Yves Montand set the pace, but the person who brought it instant fame was Piaf. When Piaf sang in the Club des Cinq the place became a night-club again. It was full to bursting; people even sat on the stairs.

It was 10.00 p.m. – time for Piaf to come on. The curtain went up and she appeared: delicate, thin, fragile. To boost her confidence she always wore the same black dress. She had made it for her début out of some cut-price balls of wool. She had a way of turning the most ordinary song into a memorable experience. The words were totally convincing when she sang them. Her songs were about poverty, loneliness, fleeting love, hope and misery, all of which she had experienced. She was a musician who knew nothing about music but had an extraordinary

29

feeling for it. Whatever she sang the audiences would respond warmly: whether it was *'L'accordéoniste'*, *'De l'autre côté de la rue'* or *'J' m'en fous pas mal'*. She would sing eight songs on her own and then one with the Compagnons de la Chanson. It wouldn't have been the same song without her. It was called *'Les trois cloches'* ('The three bells') and has been engraved for ever on the hearts of the masses. There was a story attached to it. It all began with a remark Piaf made to her sister, Simone Berteaut, 'Momone' as she was called, who had sung with her in the streets: 'You have no idea what *"cloches"* (dullards) those Compagnons are!' Edith had said it in the sharp, exasperated tone of someone who couldn't bear to waste time. And as far as she was concerned, the Compagnons were undoubtedly wasting time.

Refugees from various youth movements in which they were no longer comfortable, the Compagnons met up by chance in Lyons during the Occupation. It was chance again which introduced them to their lucky star, Piaf. And their luck was personified by their mascot, a delightful little wooden chick, Bobby, which they took with them everywhere, since their first tour with Edith in Germany in the spring. They were nine happy-go-lucky young men ranging in age from twenty to twenty-eight, and in height from five to six foot. Only Paul, the youngest, was from Paris. The rest came from the provinces. Apart from Fred, perhaps, who had cultivated what had always been an extremely pure voice, none of them had really intended to become singers.

Jean-Louis Jaubert, who was the brains of the group, had been a trainee in a bank. Guy Bourguignon, who acted as cook and stage manager, had lost interest in law before he even started. He had wanted to become an actor. For a time he had been with a group of travelling players. The redhead in the group, Albert, a comic mime, was forever performing acrobatic feats; he had previously earned his living this way. The others – Jo Frachon, who pretended to be half-asleep on stage but managed to fight it off in real life; Hubert, who didn't take anything seriously; and Gérard, whose hobby was collecting radios and who wore vulgar, jazzy ties – were all former students who had finally found their feet.

When Edith met them they were only singing to high-class audiences. Their repertoire was based on traditional French songs and country airs. They only sang in provincial theatres, as though this was their natural milieu. Then Edith burst into their lives, all sauce and cheeky humour. Their polite manners and choirboy songs amused her. She would listen to them and say: 'Well done, chaps, but if you want to make a career out of it, it might be better to change your style.'

Jaubert was originally against this idea on the grounds that the Compagnons should stick to choral singing.

'Fine,' was Edith's retort. 'But I'm beginning to get tired of your "crocuses in the fields".'

Determined to make them famous in spite of themselves, she insisted that they should change.

They would say, 'But Edith, we don't want fame.'

'Then you're bloody fools,' she would reply.

The 'bloody fools' finally saw it was in their interests and gave in. After their brief tour, fifteen days in Germany as a trial run, she handed them Paris, the Club des Cinq and 'Les trois cloches' on a plate. This song, written by Gilles, had been going through Edith's head for some time. One morning she sang it to all nine of them. When she came to the end she asked them what they thought of it. As they didn't know what Edith had in mind they were reserved in their comments. But Jaubert wasn't keen: 'No, Edith. It's not us.'

'I see. How would it be if I were to sing it with you?'

31

It was immediately obvious to the Compagnons that it would work very well. It was, in fact, a sure winner. And that was how the bell in the song came to ring out: '*Que sa voix d'écho en écho, a dit au monde qui s'étonne, c'est pour Jean-François Nicot . . .*' ('Its echoing voice told the surprised world it was ringing for Jean-François Nicot . . .').

That evening, Cerdan was dining in the Club des Cinq with Jo Longman and a few friends. He still bore the marks of the fight against Robert Charron that had been attended by throngs of Parisians in the Parc des Princes. He was at home in the Club and had developed his own routine there. It was Jo's scene. Cerdan often sat at the same table, on the left, and watched the stage.

The odd thing was that Lucien Roupp was sitting at another table. He wasn't in Cerdan's corner that evening. But perhaps this was all Jo's doing as well. The Cerdan-Longman relationship was beginning to look like a conspiracy. Perhaps Roupp sensed some kind of danger and the risk of losing Cerdan one day.

Everything had happened very fast in the last few months for Marcel. He was beginning to see Paris with the eyes of a Parisian. He was dazzled by everything that sparkled. And that evening it was Piaf.

Carried away by her singing, Marcel clapped longer than anyone else. He wanted to show how much he had liked her. He wasn't the sort of person who liked to make himself the centre of attention. It was simply in his nature to go straight for anything good or beautiful. And as far as he was concerned, Piaf's performance was beautiful.

He turned back to Jo. 'She's wonderful.'

Danièle Vigneaud who was sitting at his table smiled. Marcel's spontaneous remark made her confide to him: 'I know her well, you know.'

Danièle had unwittingly made herself the centre of attention. She was extremely reserved and shy by nature. It was too late. Marcel wanted to know more. He pressed her: 'You know her?'

Danièle, who was later to become Mme Marc Bonel, told them about her past. At the age of three she had acted in a film; her uncle was an assistant film director. She had appeared at the opening of the Empire Theatre. The good-natured and fatherly Maurice Chevalier had taken a liking to her and shown her around the wings. She had gone on to become a good *corps de ballet* dancer. She had even appeared in *Violettes Impériales*.

'I met Edith in 1940 when she was on at the Amiral. I was on the same bill.'

Cerdan wanted to know more. 'But is she a friend of yours?'

Danièle was embarrassed. She was afraid she had exaggerated. Straightforward, modest person that she was, she corrected herself. 'Oh no! You know what I mean. If I meet her she greets me. That's as far as it goes.'

The fact of the matter was that Edith had always liked Danièle for one very simple reason: she had never been one to flirt with men. That very evening with Cerdan, Danièle was happily taking a back seat. She had come to please her friend Denise, a beautiful woman who was then a member of Cerdan's circle in Paris and whose looks Cerdan had already noticed.

Jo Longman managed to bring the attention back to himself. The curtain had gone down after Piaf's last song *'La vie en rose'*. Longman took the opportunity to create a bit of a stir. 'Marcel, would you like me to introduce you?'

Longman disappeared into the wings without waiting for an answer. In less than a quarter of an hour she tottered up on her built-up shoes, a look of amusement on her face. When Jo had suggested that she join Marcel

Cerdan's table she had smiled. 'A boxer? Well, that will make a change.'

But that wasn't the only surprise in store for her. As far as she was concerned, a boxer was simply a pair of shoulders, a square build and a strong grip. And now she could see for herself the man whom Jo had described as much more than this.

'Edith. Let me introduce you to Marcel Cerdan.'

And here he was face to face with Piaf. He was intimidated and embarrassed. What on earth was he going to say to her? That she was marvellous? That she had a nice voice? It sounded silly. She'd been told that a hundred times before. And now everyone in the place was looking at him, at them, full of curiosity.

'Congratulations! You're very good at what you do,' she said to him. It wasn't much but she meant it.

In the end, it just came out. He was cross with himself but he couldn't help telling her: 'You have a magnificent voice.'

Luckily, Edith suddenly recognised Danièle. They started up a brief conversation. Cerdan was saved.

Edith ordered a tomato juice. She looked into the boxer's eyes for a second. 'Me too,' he said without thinking. All of a sudden, Cerdan's table had become Piaf's table. People elbowed each other and squeezed up, inundating her with questions. She told them she was on top form and that life could be great sometimes. Her eyes were full of laughter.

Marc Bonel, Edith's accordionist, arrived.

'Come here, darling, and sit with us,' said Piaf invitingly.

He knew every one of Edith's songs and every contest Cerdan had fought. Despeaux, KO fifth round; Menozzi, KO third round; Tenet, victory on points; Tom Davies, KO first round; Diouf, KO third round. And Guedes in

Lisbon, KO first round; Tenet again, victory on points; and Ferrer in Barcelona, KO fourth round. It was impossible to catch Bonel out. Cerdan had always been his idol and Piaf was his fairy godmother.

Like her, he had had a poverty-stricken childhood. He had turned to the accordion as a means of survival. And he had struck lucky. In the middle of the war he had been called up to play in the Théâtre des Armées. He was stationed in Saint Dizier. One day, Fernandel passed through. He needed another number for his programme. Bonel, who played in the barrack room, volunteered to fill the gap. Until demobilisation, he followed Fernandel everywhere. After the Liberation, Mistinguett was performing in the Alhambra. She needed an accordionist to play a piece under a gas lamp. He was there at the time and found himself propelled on to the stage. Eight days later, Piaf took Mistinguett's place. Her Belgian accordionist stood her up. So Bonel, who was always around, got a second chance. He was told to get in touch with Robert Chauvigny, Piaf's pianist and orchestrator who lived in the rue d'Orsel in Montmartre. Chauvigny made him play a piece and then gave him some scores to practise. His face was a picture: 'But I don't know anything about music.'

He worked on it for two whole days and nights. Eventually he was introduced to Piaf. Bonel would never forget the meeting. He would always remember Edith turning to Chauvigny: 'Robert, who on earth is this? Look at him!'

Six months later Bonel was calling Piaf 'sweetie'. And thanks to her, here he was this evening, sitting next to Cerdan. He asked him: 'Was it really so hard against Charron?'

'Yes, yes,' confessed Cerdan. 'I wasn't accurate enough and I got very short of breath.'

'The press certainly didn't make it sound easy . . .'

35

Cerdan was too distracted to reply, because Edith was getting up to leave. She made her apologies: she had to go. She held out her hand and, without thinking, he heard himself say: 'See you soon.'

She was meeting Jean-Louis Jaubert, *her* Compagnon.

4

A Night in New York

They had been turning people away every evening for
the last week at the Théâtre de l'Etoile. All 1,300 seats
were booked. The show, which was presented by Jacques
Dutal, began with Roche and Aznavour. Clifford C.
Fischer thought this opening number was only 'so-so'.
An American of German origin, Fischer had just arrived
in Paris (September 1947). He was an important figure in
the world of show business; all doors were open to him
– he represented Broadway, and Broadway is the hub of
show business. Although physically on the round side,
he was a sharp businessman who set the trend for New
York shows.

He sat in one of the front rows. One of his friends had
mentioned Piaf's name to him. Edith had just been given
a triumphant reception in Scandinavia. The show marked
her return to Paris. Fischer had come along to decide for
himself.

He sat through the whole show, and thought Luc
Barney a 'personable singer'; the singer and dancer Irene
de Trébert had 'good style'; the English pair George and
Tim Dormonde who brought the house down with
laughter performed 'interesting acrobatic clowning'; and
the Greek dancers Lyda and Yani Alma had 'nice style'.
The next on were the Compagnons de la Chanson.

They were excellent, not just because of the sound they

37

produced, which the critics thought was no more than 'good', but because of their skill at mime, their sense of irony, the fact that they were all 'nice' boys, their visual impact, their interaction as a group, and their flair for French songs. The Compagnons had a sort of infectious lightheartedness that made you feel love would always find a way; that the world was full of maids with captivating figures and men who were never short of lines to make them laugh or win their favours. And the Compagnons didn't just put it across in an old-fashioned way. They knew how to make the most of it and bring out the meaning of what they were singing: they would screw up their faces and contort their bodies, like gargoyles. Fischer was completely won over.

Piaf came on next. She sang nine songs. Fischer was dazzled. After the show, Piaf gathered the Compagnons together and told them: 'Boys, I think we're beginning to get somewhere. We're going to be auditioned by someone important.'

A rendezvous was arranged for the next afternoon in Countess Pastré's house in the Latin Quarter. Piaf, the Compagnons, Loulou Barrier, Marc Bonel and Robert Chauvigny sat waiting for Fischer in nervous anticipation.

Fischer made a dramatic entrance. He rushed over to Robert Chauvigny and held him in a long embrace, repeating over and over again, 'My dear Robert'. Edith was taken aback. She thought that Fischer had come mainly to hear her, yet he only seemed to have eyes and ears for her pianist. Why?

She was soon to find out. Fischer had worked with Robert before the war when he was conducting an orchestra of a hundred musicians in New York. He was equally competent on the piano, the violin and the cello.

Edith couldn't get over it. She grew impatient and her irritation began to show. And then they were ready to start. The audition began. Fischer took a seat at the back of the room. He was treated to a full programme of songs. When they had finished he took off his glasses, wiped his eyes and said: 'Thank you. It was beautiful. I've never heard anything so good.' But he had one reservation: 'I'm afraid, however, that it might be too beautiful for the Americans. That's why I think it might be too soon to bring you to Broadway.'

It was decided to hold a second audition. Fischer needed time to think. His instinct told him that he shouldn't rush Piaf's American career, but nor should he let the opportunity slip. He weighed up the pros and cons and decided to go ahead. The contract was signed. Piaf and the Compagnons were to appear for four and a half weeks at the Playhouse Theatre in New York.

Edith couldn't contain her happiness as the date of departure drew near. To get herself ready for America she went the rounds of the great Parisian couturiers (Balmain, Heim, etc.) with her secretary, Ginou. The fittings went on for ever. Nothing was too beautiful or too expensive. Madame Paul, the head seamstress at Heim, developed a liking for Edith. Ginou was still a bit shy. Edith put her at her ease. She asked her what she thought about all the dresses she tried on. She kept telling her: 'Ginou, sweetheart, bear in mind that we're going to be representing France and that we must be very elegant.' On the spur of the moment, Ginou cut her long, straight brown hair and Edith made her pluck her eyebrows.

Edith deserted her temporarily on the boat. Each according to their station: Piaf, Jaubert and Barrier travelled first class; Ginou, the musicians and the other Compagnons went second class. And there was Edith's surprise guest: her old friend Irene de Trébert, who had also been performing since an early age. At five, Irene was dancing in the Gaumont Palace in Place Clichy to the sounds of

Enoch Light's American orchestra. At seven she went to the Opéra, a child prodigy ballerina who was to become a star. Later on she was given the name Riri Colibri, and at fourteen she took the plunge and went to America. She spent three years at the French Casino in New York. During this time she built up her reputation, was talent-spotted and appeared in the film *Mademoiselle Swing*.

Piaf entered her life in 1939. Irene was performing at the Amiral with Paul Meurisse. Piaf was just starting in the club next door, the Night Club. On the evening of her première performance, Irene took Meurisse to give Edith moral support. They all had dinner together with a group of friends at La Cloche d'Or in rue Mansart, at the bottom of La Butte – a restaurant that stayed open late for performers. At the end of the meal, Meurisse offered to take Edith home. Their meeting that evening developed into an affair. Irene decided to keep her distance. Edith and Irene didn't meet up again until the summer of 1946, in Greece. Irene had been drawing the crowds for the last few weeks in an open-air cabaret in Athens. When she heard of Edith's imminent arrival she was delighted and decided to go and meet her. They were soon appearing on the same posters and in front of the same audiences.

The Greeks who went crazy over Irene's buxom, blonde beauty, laughed at Edith's little face and black dress. So scornful were they that some members of the audience even threw coins at her feet, a sign of extreme contempt. Outraged, Irene de Trébert rushed up to Edith and dragged her off into the wings. She returned on her own and told the audience in a firm, but furious voice, 'I don't think you quite understand who Edith Piaf is. Let her sing and you'll see.'

As a result, Edith in turn scored a success in Athens. Edith and Irene became inseparable. In Paris, Edith insisted that she should be on the programme at the Etoile Theatre.

As Irene de Trébert recalls:

'When Edith told me she was leaving for New York I was happy for her sake but a bit sad to lose her. I was in a bad way that day as I had had a setback over a musical arrangement which Raymond Legrand had promised me. He had arranged to meet me in the Salle Gaveau at four. He stood me up. So I just left and went to look for Edith. She was waiting for a composer. She was bubbling over with excitement and said to me: "Have you got any lipstick on you?" I held out my bag. Edith rummaged through it and came across a little revolver which I had just bought.

' "What on earth are you doing with this?" she said.

' "It's to kill Raymond Legrand with."

' "Are you mad?"

'I never found out whether she believed me or not but she decided that I had to be taken away from Paris. She telephoned Maurice Chevalier, who had some pull in the American Embassy, and asked him to get me a visa.

'In the meantime she got in touch with my mother, who packed a trunk of clothes. I didn't know anything about it. The big day arrived, and she said: "Come with us to Le Havre." So I did. Saint-Lazare station was full of photographers and reporters. Edith and the Compagnons were made to climb up on top of the luggage-trolleys. It was all great fun. I was going to leave them in Le Havre but Edith made me get on the boat. I was still on it when the boat left.'

Edith didn't really enjoy eating lunch at the captain's table

– thank goodness Irene was there – but Edith put on a brave face and did what was expected of her.

At last they reached New York.

Edith expected to be dazzled by America, but she never got over the feeling of being a fish out of water. The Statue of Liberty in New York harbour had no more effect on her than the statue in front of the Mirabeau Bridge in Paris. What really hit her about New York were the streets, where the pedestrians were always in a hurry, eternally late, as if they were constantly trying to cut down on the time it took them to get from home to office and back again. Edith commented: 'My word, they're all Ladoumègues – every one an athlete.'

Edith insisted that Irene share her room at the Ambassador Hotel. She walked over to the window and with a tired movement gestured towards the view of New York. 'You know, these skyscrapers scare the pants off me. They're so gigantic; it's all too much.'

She wasn't at home in this world. She already longed for Paris in the way people long for water in the middle of the Sahara. Her homesickness for the banks of the Seine coloured her response to New York. Irene was always cheerful and ready for anything, but Edith was lonely in America, even with Irene, and on one occasion she sang Vincent Scotto's old song to herself:

> 'Y'en a qui vous parlent de l'Amérique
> Ils ont des visions de cinéma.
> Ils vous disent: quel pays magnifique . . .
> . .Où est-il donc mon moulin de la place Blanche
> Mon tabac et mon bistro du coin.
> Où sont-ils les amis, les copains?'

('People talk about America/They have visions from the movies/They tell you it's a magnificent country/But where is my Moulin Rouge on the Place Blanche/My corner shop, my local bistro?/Where are my friends, my pals?')

Edith didn't take easily to life in New York. She came up against a barrier higher than all the skyscrapers which surrounded and oppressed her: the English language. She tried hard to make light of the problem by laughing during her first press conference, particularly over the pronunciation of her name. She had been warned in advance that her name (pronounced 'Aydeet' in French) was pronounced differently in America. But it had still made her laugh. She had also played along when the same journalists had asked her who she wanted to meet in America. She pretended to think it over. 'Einstein,' she cried out. It was the first name that had come to mind, and it went down very well. There were even more laughs when Piaf, knowing she was on to a good thing, added: 'While you're about it, why don't you give me his telephone number?'

But it was uphill all the way after this. It was all very well having Jean-Louis Jaubert act as official interpreter: on the basis of the one year of English he had done ten years ago he proudly produced a few catch-all phrases. Edith developed a complex about it. She convinced herself that English wasn't for her and vice versa.

Clifford Fischer and Loulou Barrier were forced to intervene and ensure that somehow or other Edith managed to overcome the language barrier. She took on an English teacher, Miss Davidson, a spinster with a bun who taught at Columbia University. One of her major feats was to have knocked the rough edges off Luis Mariano's Franco-Andalusian accent, and teach him to speak good American. At the same time Piaf threw herself whole-heartedly, if somewhat joylessly, into a little book called

43

L'Anglais Sans Peine (English without Tears) which became her bedside reading.

The Americans were tickled by an account in the *New Yorker* of a journalist's visit to Piaf in her apartment in the Ambassador Hotel:

> 'When I got there at one o'clock Edith Piaf had just woken up. I was waiting in the sitting-room while she dressed when I noticed some notes scribbled in pencil next to a book called *L'Anglais Sans Peine*. It was open at the chapter entitled "Pronounciation of the English 'th'." The notes were in English. It was obviously an introduction to the songs that Piaf was going to sing in French. I can only conclude she's learning it off by heart.'

Edith was still feeling somewhat lost in New York when she received a phone call from some French fans of hers who ran an inn thirty-odd miles from New York. She brightened up when they told her: 'We'd be delighted if you'd come to lunch. If you can make it, a car will come and pick you up at your hotel.'

Edith turned to Irene: 'Shall we go? It would make a change, wouldn't it?' Naturally enough, Irene agreed.

The next day, which was a Sunday, they found themselves in the back of a movie-style limousine driving through Manhattan. Being the weekend, the place was deserted. The car drove along the Hudson River, crossed the outskirts of the Bronx and stopped in a slightly rustic hamlet in the middle of a big park. This was the village of Congers, situated in the centre of a region dotted with lakes, where about thirty French families had established themselves. The car was parked in front of a little hotel-restaurant called Chez Jean. The young owners, a warm and welcoming couple called the Gallis, were standing on the steps. They were visibly moved to have Piaf come to their home. It was a big day. Piaf's visit brought half of France under their roof. The other half was already there – Cerdan.

'Marcel Cerdan? Here?' Edith was stunned.

'Yes, madame. It's a great honour for us.'

Piaf nudged Irene. 'Fancy finding him here.'

The Gallis told her he was between two fights. The first had been a success. He had defeated Billy Walker in two minutes forty seconds in Montreal, and he was training nearby for his match at the end of the month in Chicago against Anton Raadik.

There were ten of them for lunch. Cerdan was obviously pleased to find himself next to Irene de Trébert. In fact Irene felt his knee touch hers several times, but she kept apologising, pretending it was an accident. However, she decided to change places with Edith on a trifling pretext: 'Edith, I need a bit of air. Could I take your place by the window?'

Edith jumped at the chance. Cerdan's presence had put her in very good spirits. Irene, who knew her well, had noticed.

Edith didn't have a clue about boxing, but you didn't need to have been to the Vélodrome d'Hiver to be able to say to Cerdan in 1947, 'You're doing a great job. We're proud of you.' The meal was a success and ended on a good note.

That evening in their bedroom at the Ambassador, Irene quizzed Edith. 'Did you enjoy yourself?' Irene asked her, looking a bit peeved.

'Oh yes. That Cerdan . . .'

'You don't mean to tell me . . .'

'What do you think?' Edith exclaimed, her eyes sparkling. 'But you saw him. What a man!'

Irene got the picture. She wasn't surprised when Edith

added: 'Anyway, we're having dinner together tomorrow night.' She paused and then, looking Irene in the eye, she asked her: 'You'll come with us, won't you?'

The next evening Irene pulled out. She went to see a musical comedy on Broadway with Jacques Pills. He was married to Lucienne Boyer, who was also singing in New York. Edith, who was usually all too quick to berate her friends if she thought they preferred someone else's company let it pass that time. 'Well, if you'd enjoy it . . . Do as you like.'

Irene de Trébert dined out after the show and didn't come back until very late that evening. Jacques Pills accompanied her back to the hotel. When she entered the bedroom she was careful not to turn on the light or make any noise. She took her shoes off out of consideration for her friend. Edith was a very light sleeper, and had lots of nightmares. Irene often had to hold her in her arms to calm her down. In spite of her earplugs and an eye-mask, Edith would wake up at the slightest sound.

When she got into bed, Irene heard a sigh. She turned the light on, thinking Edith was having another nightmare. It would have been better if she had turned the light on when she first came in. At least she would have got the picture straight away. They were both there. Irene took her pillow and blanket and settled down to spend the night in the sitting-room.

Edith appeared not to have noticed. In the morning while she was warming up Marcel's coffee she seemed amazed to see Irene. 'What are you doing here?' she asked.

5

Chicago–Broadway: a Ring and a Stage

Marcel, 31 October 1947, Chicago
The scales put Cerdan at the lower limit for the middle-weight category: 160 pounds. Raadik was more than a pound heavier. The weighing-in had been presided over by Harold Ryan, Chief Inspector of the Illinois Boxing Commission. After a final medical examination, Marcel admitted how important it was to him to do well in this fight as he expected it to be the last before the world championship.

During his recent training sessions in Marigold Garden, Cerdan had seemed on top form. But the press couldn't help noticing that he now looked poorly – a bad sign, particularly since he also seemed to be lacking his usual self-confidence. Was he afraid of Anton Raadik, who gave every appearance of being a brawler, with his icy gaze, flat nose and square jaw and his many years' experience? But no, it had nothing to do with fear.

If Cerdan looked worried at midday it was because he was emotionally upset. He had just heard that one of his brothers-in-law had died. Louis Lopez was only twenty-two and Cerdan had been very fond of him. He took the news badly, like a blow below the belt.

He rested for a while after the weighing-in and then went out for lunch. Jo Rizzo took them to L'Aiglon, a good French restaurant in Chicago. Marcel and Roupp had invited three French journalists: Robert Bré, Georges Peeters and Jean Kroutchtein. They were served enormous T-bone steaks, with green vegetables. The steak was covered with a thick, dark sauce. Marcel tucked into the slab of meat without thinking and ignored Jo Rizzo's warnings to him to watch what he ate. He even had an egg flip. When they left the restaurant, Rizzo and Roupp expected Marcel to take them to a local cinema as he usually did. But on this occasion he chose to go back to the hotel after a stroll through Lincoln Park. He spent the next three hours lying down in his bedroom, staring at the ceiling, before they left for Chicago Stadium.

The packs of cards came out, as usual, as soon as they got into the dressing-rooms. Cerdan lost, which was not so usual. Rizzo was the first to register his surprise. Roupp even asked them to stop the game.

'Marcel, what's the matter? Is something wrong?'

'Everything's fine, Mr Roupp. . . .'

Edith, the same evening, on Broadway

The curtain went up on the Playhouse stage. The programme at this famous theatre on 48th Street included George and Tim Dormonde, who had appeared at the Etoile Theatre, the Canovas, Lyda Alma and Vanni Fleury, and the Winter Sisters. Dorritt Merrill introduced the show, which was presented by George-Henri Martin. Clifford C. Fischer was the producer.

The Playhouse was synonymous with the name of a great American actress. Miss Grace George always came to mind when people talked about the theatre. She was responsible for setting up the cabaret in the spring of 1911.

The show opened with the acrobats. The magician was next and then George and Tim Dormonde. The vast stage provided plenty of room for them to perform their bicycle number. They were followed by Greek dancers, and two strong Italian weight-lifters who rolled their muscles and clowned about to amuse the crowd.

The Compagnons were next. They came across very well. They sang in French, but the fact that no one in the audience understood didn't seem to matter. Their parody of '*Au clair de la lune*' was greeted with loud applause. They gave it three different treatments: it was sung in the style of a New Orleans jazz band, Russian style, and with all the solemnity of a symphony orchestra. This perform-ance won the Compagnons a tribute from the *New York Herald Tribune* illustrator and a rave review in *Newsweek*:

> 'They can't put a foot wrong. For the last two years they have been touring with Piaf and are undoubt-edly the freshest and most original group to have surfaced for years. They sing in French but they would be just as entertaining in whatever language they chose to perform.'

The Compagnons' last song was '*Les trois cloches*'. Edith came on in her black dress, all of four feet eleven inches, and dominated the ensemble. The audience was transfixed. People looked at each other in surprise as if to say: 'So this is Piaf!'

Cerdan was normally pale when the bell went. This time he was positively yellow. Something was wrong. The fight began and although an invisible force seemed to propel him to the centre of the ring his opponent, Raadik, was the first to attack. He produced a classic left jab followed by a right hook which failed to connect. Cerdan responded by hitting out angrily. He delivered a series of hooks. Raadik was unmoved.

'*La madelon*' was played during the interval before the

second round. Raadik was the first back in the ring. The Estonian had a tendency to hit too wide. Cerdan tried to go into a clinch, elbowing him. The referee had to caution him. Now Cerdan was on the attack with uppercuts and hooks. He managed to hit Raadik hard but his attack came too late and the bell went. Cerdan could have done with a slightly longer round.

Third round: Cerdan launched a new attack. A right hook to Raadik's jaw. There were shouts from the audience and their voices reflected the emotion behind the violent fight. It seemed clear that Cerdan had almost completed his efforts to destroy Raadik. Raadik was bleeding; he had a cut above the eye.

But why were people whistling? Edith didn't understand. She looked at Jean-Louis Jaubert, who remained impassive. Edith still didn't understand. It was the first time this had happened to her. If she had had the courage, she would have told them to go to hell! As far as she was concerned they would never understand anything. Only later was she to learn what it meant. In the United States people always whistle, even when they like something. But it seemed very odd to her.

The Compagnons spent the interval revelling in their success. The dressing-rooms were loud with their joyous exuberance. They had made an instant impact on the audience. Edith did not know what to make of it. When she heard Clifford Fischer tell her in an encouraging, paternal voice, 'Edith, it's your turn,' she knew it was not going to be easy. She realised what a struggle it would be singing to this audience for whom she had no feeling.

She had had two of her songs translated, 'La vie en rose' and 'Bonjour Monsieur Saint-Pierre', and had learned the English versions by heart. She had not been terribly enthusiastic about the idea, but Clifford Fischer kept telling her, 'Don't forget, Edith, it's a different kind of audience.' She gave in.

There were four other songs in her repertoire: '*J' m'en fous pas mal*', '*La mariée*', '*L'accordéoniste*' and '*Mon légionnaire*'.

The first two songs in English went down well, but the Master of Ceremonies started explaining the other songs over the microphone. It was a disaster. The audience sat through the whole of her performance without understanding a single word of what Piaf was trying to get across.

Raadik was like a rock. His stamina and ability to take a lot of beating were making it into a dramatic fight. At the beginning the spectators were on Raadik's side because they saw him as being at the 'Frenchie's' mercy. But Raadik was doing better than they had ever hoped. Not only was he standing up to the 'Moroccan Bomber' but he was trading punches blow for blow and had begun to knock Cerdan around.

Cerdan kept trying to bring the fight to an end but his punches just weren't up to it that evening. By the end of the eighth round Cerdan looked completely worn out.

Ninth round: Marcel went all out to win. He landed a right hook of unbelievable strength on Raadik's face, but Raadik seemed indestructible. The effort of delivering the blow caused Cerdan to stagger. From then on he just played for time. He looked worried . . . Perhaps he knew he wasn't fighting anywhere near as well as he could. The last twenty seconds were very difficult for him. Raadik managed to hit him with a string of hooks. When the bell went Cerdan retreated, despondent, to his corner.

The curtain fell. Edith had finished singing and all she could hear was applause. There were no more whistles –

she almost wished there were – and there were no curtain calls. Edith had hoped it would be different. If she had to choose between wild whistling and polite indifference, she would take whistling. There was a look of disillusionment on her face. America had not lived up to her dreams.

Tenth round: Cerdan only had three minutes to go . . . it seemed that in three minutes' time he would win an easy victory on points. But suddenly, out of pure exhaustion, Marcel slipped. His knee touched the ground and he took a count of three. He got up, staggering about in a daze. Raadik was ready to finish him off, and now seemed to be the right moment. He landed a hook and Cerdan was on the mat again. Raadik felt very sure of himself. Although the fight was nearly over, he seemed more and more certain that he would be able to rob Cerdan of his victory. Cerdan was down for a count of four and only got to his feet again with considerable difficulty. He clung to Raadik, then fell down again in exhaustion. In his corner Roupp, with his eye on the stop-watch, pleaded with him to get up. Through sheer will-power, Marcel made another enormous effort and pulled himself up. He was unsteady and had to hold onto the ropes. He was wrecked and only half-conscious for the last few seconds of the fight.

The bell went. He didn't hear it. The referee turned to the two judges. There was no discussion: Cerdan was unanimously declared the winner.

He made his way back to the dressing-room on legs that could hardly hold him up. He collapsed on to the massage table. Lew Burston, Lucien Roupp and Jo Longman closed the door behind them. No one was going to be allowed to see the pitiful sight of a broken Marcel. He remained stretched out for more than an hour. His eyes were dull. A doctor appeared, and showed concern about Marcel's vomiting. No one dared tell him the state he was in when he went into the ring.

When he had recovered, Cerdan turned towards Lucien Roupp, who had been his manager for so long. He shook his head, his eyes filled with tears: 'I'm finished, Mr Roupp, finished.'

In New York, Piaf had suffered a similar body blow. She rejected the rather forced compliments paid her by Clifford Fischer and Loulou Barrier. She was sad – sad for herself and for them. 'They didn't understand a thing,' she said. 'It must be my fault. Why on earth should they want to listen to my songs? They want to be happy and I remind them of people who are sad. I sing about poverty and despair. What an idiot I am! As as for that twit who only made matters worse by trying to explain what I was singing about . . .'

All Edith could think about that evening was packing her bags and taking the first boat home.

Cerdan didn't hang around long in Chicago. The day after the fight, a Saturday, he caught the plane back to New York. He had a pathetic look about him, in strong contrast to Roupp's understandable sense of satisfaction. Cerdan may have been knocked about a bit but he had won the fight against Raadik.

Marcel was still smarting from all the punches he had taken, and he had had trouble getting to sleep. He kept turning things over in his mind. He dreaded reading the American press. Wrongly so, because, as it turned out, the Chicago papers praised his courage and, like the judges, were unanimous about his victory, giving him seven, eight or even nine rounds out of ten. It was the correspondents of the French papers who were to be the most critical. Of course, no one actually criticised the boxer who had already given so much, but the tone was reserved and there were endless insinuations about the way in which he had prepared for the fight, and Roupp's and Burston's irresponsibility in not keeping a close eye on him.

It was no good Cerdan talking about 'extenuating circumstances': 'Don't be too hard on me. I was suffering from indigestion before I went into the ring and I admit that I wasn't as fit as usual in the fight against Raadik.' A few well-informed French journalists, such as Georges Février, writing in the *Miroir-Sprint*, were not prepared to be kind.

'How could Roupp and Burston have let Cerdan make such a serious mistake as to eat a rich meat dish and then follow it with an egg-flip just a few hours before the fight?

'And didn't our champion say that he had only sparred eight times by way of preparation for the fight against Raadik, and that he had sometimes gone without his morning run?

'Marcel was certainly not well. But it would seem he was to blame; he hadn't taken his preparation seriously enough.

'I know that he has been hard at it for the last twelve years and that the role of super-champion is a gruelling one to maintain. Any man can have moments of weakness – it's only human. But what is inexcusable is that this should result from a few days of easy living or inadequate training.

'Quite apart from his duty as a French sportsman, Marcel should bear in mind that a few slip-ups of this kind could deprive him of the opportunity to fight for the world title. This is what Roupp and Burston should be telling him every day. . . .'

Février didn't mince his words. But Marcel hadn't really jeopardised his chances. Immediately after his victory against Raadik, Abe Green, President of the National Boxing Association, sent him a telegram: 'Cerdan Graziano's number one challenger for the world championship.'

In the plane to New York there was the inevitable post-mortem which follows every fight. Cerdan was used to it, but this time his mind was elsewhere. He leaned back in his seat and closed his eyes. His mind was on Edith and something she had said the other evening in New York. One sentence in particular was beginning to haunt him: 'Marcel, you must get used to the idea that you're not always going to win.' Edith had not meant to be unkind and Marcel had taken it in the spirit in which she intended it, but he hadn't fully appreciated the warning at the time.

'You see, Mr Roupp, she was right.'

Roupp turned round in surprise. 'Oh, so you're not asleep!'

Cerdan went on: 'No, I was thinking about something Edith said to me.'

'Oh yes, and what was that?'

'Nothing, nothing, except that the time has come for me to start thinking about losing. It only occurred to me in the tenth round.'

Roupp spent the rest of the flight lecturing Cerdan about not listening to people who didn't know the first thing about boxing, however celebrated they might be in their own field; they should mind their own business. Marcel shrugged his shoulders and said nothing.

When they arrived in New York he wanted to see Edith as soon as possible. She would help him escape his mood of depression. He didn't know – how could he have guessed? – that Edith had been something of a flop at the

Playhouse, that she too had taken a beating of a sort. She was so sure they would like her, that she would have the Americans eating out of her hand, but she was wrong: it was not so easy. She had had more than her share of bad reviews. With her little black dress, style-less hair-do, her pale face, her performance on stage – what performance? – she had been a disaster.

That was clearly not the case as far as the Compagnons were concerned.

'Well done, darlings. I'm very happy for you,' she said, meaning it. But she had hoped for a little more consideration from them than she got. Things were not going too smoothly between her and Jean-Louis Jaubert. Jaubert had distanced himself from Edith, both the singer and the woman, and in Paris tongues would soon be wagging.

Marcel's arrival on the scene was opportune. Edith needed him, but the strong man she had met before had turned into someone riddled with self-doubt. She couldn't help laughing: here she was with a winner who acted as though he were a loser. She was amazed, and she forgot her own disillusionment. When they dined together she asked him, 'Well, Marcel, you won, didn't you? So what are you complaining about?'

Edith had read the fairly complimentary accounts of his fight against Raadik. All he had looked at and taken in were the photos. Cerdan down – that was news. And the photographers loved it.

'You see, photos like that hurt,' he said in his shrill voice. 'It's the first time I've been down in more than a hundred fights.' He was in despair. There were tears in his eyes.

Edith refused to hear any more: 'You're talking nonsense! Would you rather be in Raadik's shoes? Read the papers.'

'I've seen them, Edith.'

'You haven't looked at them properly. Read what they say about you: "For the first time after more than a hundred fights, Cerdan is down." ' She showed her impatience and added: 'Don't you think it's the best tribute you've ever been paid?'

She wanted to sweep away all his uncertainty with an irrefutable argument, a brush of the hand. All she managed to do was to lessen Marcel's disappointment at having botched his fight against Raadik. Past fights which he thought had disappeared for ever returned to haunt him. The names of Humery and Viez rang through his head. They were painful memories.

'What's the matter, Marcel?' Edith asked anxiously.

'I'm fed up with boxing.'

'Fed up?'

'Yes, really fed up. And not for the first time. I wanted to chuck it all in before.'

'Are you crazy?'

Marcel decided to face some of the skeletons in his past. After all, Edith wasn't going to go round telling everyone. He got carried away. She listened. He began by talking about Humery.

Humery was a good guy in everyday life but an animal in the ring. The first time they fought Cerdan told himself, 'Marcel, watch out, he's a tough nut. You may get more than you bargained for.' That's exactly what happened. It went on for five rounds . . . five rounds in which he was attacked from all sides. In his corner, Roupp kept telling him to keep his guard up. And then Humery started landing punishing blows to the body. Finally, in the sixth round he told himself: 'Marcel, it's time you did something or you'll come out of this badly.' He concentrated his attack on Humery's supposedly weak chin. The effect was immediate and Marcel won by a knock-out. He was pleased, particularly as Humery had said he would finish him before the sixth round. Now all he could think of was getting his revenge. But Cerdan wasn't in any great hurry . . .

Edith sat there wide-eyed and let him tell the story. She hung on his every word. She wanted to know what happened.

'He wanted his revenge and he got it. But in the meantime I had prepared myself and decided that if he wanted to fight me again, well I'd give him something to remember me by.'

Poor Humery.

'It was in the Vélodrome d'Hiver, in the spring of '42. The spectators hardly had time to sit down. I don't quite know what happened. It lasted 23 seconds including the KO. I hit him. He fell . . . 23 seconds . . . I was overjoyed at the time. But Humery stayed down. He was out cold and didn't move a muscle. He was in a coma for 45 minutes. Later, in the hospital waiting-room I paced up and down like a caged tiger. I kept asking everyone if he was going to be all right. No one would tell me. I could have wept. A boxer can do anything, but cry – never. I wanted to go into his room but they wouldn't let me. I had a terrible night. I swore that I would never go into the ring again. Humery finally pulled through, but it took a long time. When I heard he had recovered, I went down on my knees.'

Now Edith understood. They would always be on the level with one another. The dinner made her feel much better. Without any affectation, Cerdan had touched her to the heart with his spontaneity and sensitivity. He enabled her to escape from the theatricality of her world.

Cerdan went on. Edith no longer dared ask why he wanted to relive it all. He said that the next fight, three weeks later, had been even worse for him.

His opponent was Fernand Viez, thirty-six years old, a

man with more than one string to his bow. He had spent a lifetime in the ring.

'In the second round I must have hit him a bit hard. He was down for a count of nine. The spectators wanted me to finish him off. They were wild. Viez got up again. The next thing happened very quickly. He put his head on my shoulder when we were in a clinch and managed to whisper in my ear: "Don't hurt me, Marcel. I've got three kids." That really shook me.'

Edith held her head in her hands.

'There were another eight rounds to go. All I could think of was: "Marcel, whatever you do, make sure this one doesn't end up in hospital." I pretended to hit hard but it must have been a bit too obvious. Roupp asked me what Viez had said to me in the clinch. I said, "Nothing". Roupp said: "Come on, Marcel. I could see his lips moving." How could I make Roupp understand? How could I make the spectators understand? I don't think people ever whistled at me so much in the whole of my career. But you can't knock out an opponent to order, especially when he begs you not to. I felt quite sick by the end. Viez lasted ten rounds, and instead of applauding him, they whistled at me.'

The next evening, Marcel went to the Playhouse to see Edith's show. He dressed up for her. The Master of Ceremonies again provided an American commentary to Piaf's songs, and again she got annoyed, as she confessed to Marcel afterwards in the dressing-room. He replied with a nice smile, 'But you're still great. You make them happy without them even realising!'

She threw her arms round his neck in the taxi.

6

Their First Separation

Marcel, 8 November 1947, Paris
A week after his fight against Raadik, Cerdan flew to Paris where he was 'awaited', as though he owed his supporters an explanation. He was good-natured about it. His pre-arranged visit to the newspaper *Miroir-Sprint* paid dividends. He bantered with those of his supporters who were worried about what shape he was in and about his future, and he reassured them.

He was in an expansive mood. 'Chicago? I went round the abattoirs. They hang the pigs up side by side. Like this. Twenty minutes later they come out the other end in tins.'

Everyone laughed. But they pressed him. 'And Raadik, Marcel, wasn't he a hell of an opponent?'

This time Cerdan was cautious. 'I certainly didn't shine in the ring. I should have knocked him out three or four times. My punch seemed to have lost all its power.'

'And your training, Marcel?'

'Yes, it's true. I'd only done eight sessions. But I don't go for the sparring partners you get in America. They make each training session into a fight. Before fighting Abrams . . .'

'And what did you do when you found yourself on the mat?'

'I asked myself: "What on earth are you doing here,

Marcel?'' The worst thing was I couldn't get up. I got my legs to do as I told them in the end, but it was a near thing, you know.'

'And who are you going to take on next, Marcel? Graziano, Zale, or Raadik again?'

Marcel gave a big smile and replied in his shrill voice: 'Hang on, boys, I need a chance to recover. But given a choice, I'd go for Raadik. I wouldn't mind giving him something to remember me by.'

He made one last jest: 'No, I wouldn't play foul. That's not what I had in mind. But I can assure you that if I encounter him again, he won't be in the game.'

Marcel was more affected than he let on by the criticism he had received after his fight against Raadik. To cheer himself up he rushed off to the bistro run by his friend Paul Genser, at 53 rue d'Orsel at the bottom of La Butte, which he treated as his home. Friends and long-time supporters were waiting for him impatiently. Voices could be heard behind Paul's bar saying: 'It's already half past twelve. What's he up to? He won't come now. . . .' Tension was mounting. There was a constant to-ing and fro-ing between the bar and the doorway. People were straining their eyes to catch a glimpse of him in the street. There was no sign of him.

Paul was a friendly chap, with his chubby figure and big smile. He and his wife topped up glasses and tried to calm people down. 'Don't worry. He'll come. . . . It's Marcel all over.'

The telephone kept ringing. 'Paul, it's the radio people. They say Marcel had arranged to go there.'

'Tell them he'll be late, that he's been held up.'

No sooner did they put the receiver down than the phone rang again. 'Paul, someone's asking for Marcel!'

And Paul, in his jovial way, would reply: 'No, this isn't

Marcel. It's Paul. We're expecting him. He'll be here any minute.'

The same thing happened twenty or thirty times. Finally, a shout went up: 'Here he is!' Everyone rushed out onto the pavement. They all waved madly and his face lit up with a smile, but he kept going at the same pace. Before reaching the bistro, he stopped to shake hands with the grocer, the woman from the laundry and some neighbours. Marcel belonged to everyone.

As soon as he entered the café he flopped into an armchair. He answered ten questions at once, without losing his patience. He wanted to please everyone. But he didn't let it go on too long. Slowly, he got up and moved towards the kitchen. Motherly Madame Paul followed behind and asked: 'Are you hungry, Marcel? Would you like to eat straight away?'

Marcel stretched like a big cat. He threw off the jacket and tie he had put on for his public appearance and started hacking away at a gigantic steak. He was so famished he had to have two helpings.

'I'm a bit tired of the eggs and bacon they eat in the US,' he said.

Paul and Madame Genser revelled in the admission, happy and flattered to have Marcel back.

The café was deserted. From where he was sitting Marcel could see the dishevelled heads of the local kids watching his every movement from behind the curtain. They must have played truant to see him. They, too, were his fans. They were proud of their Marcel.

Later on in the evening, Marcel stretched out on a divan in the room which Paul had kept for him for ten years. Paul and Marcel's friendship went back to early January 1938. Marcel became friends with Paul after the fight against Federowich, which he won in two rounds. At the time, he was sharing a room in the hotel Aux Deux

Hémisphères in the rue des Martyrs with Martinez, whom he had once defeated. It was after that nine-round victory on 11 April 1936 that Marcel had taken home his first fantastic purse: 2,500 francs. He had come of age.

Martinez and Marcel both joined Lucien Roupp's stable in Paris at the same time. Because they had little money to spend, they found themselves frequenting modest restaurants. One lunchtime they discovered the Coq d'Or in the rue d'Orsel, where you could keep the wolf from the door for 7.25 francs, service included. And that was how Paul and Marcel became friends.

Today, Paul decided to have a heart-to-heart with Marcel. Looking embarrassed, he confided in him: 'You know, Marcel, people are saying strange things about you. Times have changed.'

He was right, old Paul, but Marcel didn't want to hear any more and cut his friend short. 'Let them talk, Paul, let them talk. . . .'

But at the other side of Paris, next to the Vélodrome d'Hiver, another famous barkeeper was neither mincing his words nor pulling his punches. It was André Routis. Twenty years earlier, in 1928, he had won the world featherweight championship, defeating Tony Canzoneri in New York on points. He was only twenty-seven at the time. Since then he had become the 'Vel' d'Hiv's' unofficial expert. From behind the bar in his bistro in rue Nélaton he would gossip with dedicated boxing fans.

The crowds would call in at Routis' establishment after getting off the overground metro at Grenelle, and eat a couple of sausages with mustard, or gulp down a glass of beer. Routis was small, with broad shoulders and a slim waist; his eyes were hidden behind thick glasses and a jutting brow. The walls of his bistro were plastered with photos of boxing highlights. The bare-chested celebrities looked down on you with their arms raised, captured for ever in the moment of victory. You had to stop off at Routis before the evening's fight to remind yourself what it was all about. His bar prepared you and he would give you his forecast with your change. And once again, Routis had no qualms about voicing his opinion. He wrote Marcel an open letter which was published in the press. The tone was both railing and falsely fraternal:

'My dear Marcel,
'Take heart. No one's going to make you fight Raadik a second time. But you will come up against other Raadiks, and you are now thirty-one. Forgive me for mentioning it. It's not your fault that the war delayed your departure for the US by five years. Things would have been different if you had taken my advice and fought Al Red Priest in Boston and earned yourself a tidy sum rather than jumping in at the deep end in Madison Square Garden. And if you had managed to win your fight with Georgie Abrams by a knock-out, your fortune would have been made. Unfortunately you had a hard time of it. It was a bad beginning, because Tony Zale or Rocky Graziano, who live in New York, won't pay any attention to you now until they see Cerdan win a clear victory over a respected boxer in New York's Madison Square Garden . . .
'While I'm still hoping for a miracle, I can't help smiling when I read the optimistic reports in the papers . . . Standing behind my bar-counter every day, I cannot help but notice how the sports crowd look up to you. I don't want to destroy this wave of mass enthusiasm, because your semi-failure against Raadik hasn't changed anything. Your setbacks in the tenth round were unfortunate but the name of Cerdan still commands respect. Whatever you do, pal, you must hang onto that!

'And if, in the near future, you were to join the crowds who come here, and tell me with that honest smile of yours which has won us all over, "My dear André, on due consideration I've decided to go home to Casablanca and settle down with my family," *I would not have the heart to dissuade you.*

'Because you would then hold the unique record of never having been defeated . . .

André Routis'

Cerdan never got to the end of the letter.

Edith, 6 December 1947, New York

'This little lady has eyes heavily ringed with mascara and a mouth big enough to swallow a quart of tomato juice in one go.'

Edith was still having no luck with the American press, but she now ignored criticism such as this, which was one of the worst examples. Yet Edith was all at sea and Marcel was a long way away. But apart from this last slap in the face, which had appeared in a satirical magazine, things were falling into place for her. It had all happened on the eve of her last appearance at the Playhouse.

Two things helped boost Edith's morale and improve her US trip. Firstly, the public now felt more kindly towards her; but more importantly, she had received an unexpected and welcome visit from Robert, the French head waiter of the fashionable Broadway night-spot, the Versailles. And the manager, Mr Provys himself, had also come along.

Robert had persuaded his boss to go and listen to Edith. He had told him that Edith's voice, gestures and physique were all part of her songs. Once people realised that a Parisienne does not always appear on stage with feathers in her hair or anywhere else, nor does she have to wear a flouncy dress, people would fight for a chance to hear Piaf sing.

Provys let himself be swayed. The timing was right. They needed a new show at the Versailles. Provys liked what he saw and heard of Piaf. He made her sign a renewable eight-day contract to start on 14 January. Although Edith kept talking of returning to France, she knew what she was doing when she tied herself to New York and the American way of life, which she continued to reject.

Irene de Trébert, who kept a close eye on her friend, day and night, had the good sense to get Edith out of the hotel, which she had started to dislike intensely. She convinced Edith to move into a very comfortable four-room apartment which she had managed to rent on the strength of her word alone, without putting down a deposit, from a rich New Yorker who spent the winter in Florida. She found it through contacts she had made in New York before the war.

It was at 891 Park Avenue, thirty blocks from the Playhouse. It was a sixteen-storey apartment block, with a narrow façade squeezed between two buildings on 78th Street. It was in a chic part of Manhattan, five minutes from the big lake in Central Park. The entrance was protected by a wide awning and opened onto a marble hall where a doorman in a white cap and gloves received visitors. Edith and Irene were on the fourth floor of this dark brick building, which was not much to look at in comparison with the buildings nearby. The apartment consisted of a small hall, cooking area, dining-room, parlour, sitting-room and two bedrooms with a bathroom.

It was almost a new life for Edith there. This time the break with the Compagnons was complete. Jean-Louis

Jaubert had not been able to resist the offers with which his group had been inundated.

'So long, boys, and good luck!' Edith told them. She saw them off, so full of self-confidence, on the first leg of their tour to Miami, where they were to parade their talents on the stage of the Latin Quarter.

Edith and the Compagnons were bound to separate one day, but Edith was still a bit upset, although she was careful not to let it show. Too bad if Guy Bourguignon was distant towards her. No doubt he had forgotten that she had paved the way for them at the Club des Cinq. It was because she had had faith in them that she had been able to get them started. As she told Jo Longman at the time: 'I promise you, I'll make these boys into stars. And if you're worried about it, I'm prepared to pay half their fee.' But that was all past history. . . .

As far as Edith was concerned, what she had to do now was to win America over, on her own. She had been lucky enough to have been offered a chance to stay a little longer. She had to make a success of it.

Irene suggested that they invite some of the most respected Broadway critics to their Park Avenue apartment. She had an ambitious plan.

'We'll treat them to some good French food. You'll see. Don't worry about the language problem, I'll translate. Just be yourself and everything will be fine.'

It was.

Irene and Edith hired Louise, from Martinique, who spoke French and was good at French cuisine, and all the guests turned up on the appointed day: Howard Barnes of the *New York Herald Tribune*; Bert McCord, who wrote the column 'Dining and Dancing'; Robert W. Dana; Dixie Tighe of the *Daily News*; Brooks Atkinson of the *New York Times*; Richard Watts Jr of the *New York Post*; and last, but not least, Vernon Rice, also of the *Post*.

Rice had really gone to town when the Playhouse show had first opened. He had made fun of Edith's broken English introduction to her songs, even giving his column a French-American heading: 'MAIS OUI, MADEMOISELLE PIAF, WE SPEAK GOOD ENGLISH!'

The meal was a lively affair, helped by good wine. Edith was simply herself, as Irene had advised, except that she handled her knife and fork with all the *savoir-faire* of a *femme du monde*; Irene de Trébert had insisted on teaching her how. People talked and joked and came away with a good impression. Indeed, three days later Edith and her friend met up with most of their guests at a big party on Fifth Avenue.

But Edith was feeling increasingly melancholic. The nights seemed endless. She kept trying to take her mind off things. She sent out and received invitations, including one from Jean Sablon who was drawing the crowds at the Waldorf Astoria. She studied English for two hours a day with Miss Davidson, and she took the air in Central Park with a short morning walk and a ritual distribution of nuts to the squirrels. But Edith was beginning to get bored. No performer enjoys the period between shows, and Piaf least of all, who couldn't survive without a stage and footlights.

Irene and Edith spent New Year's Eve in the Pavillon, a classy New York restaurant. They toasted the New Year with good French champagne – bottle after bottle. Edith lost track of how much she had had. That night she really drank. Jean-Louis Jaubert wasn't there to restrain her. Irene tried to reason with her but without success. At dawn, when they decided to return to their Park Avenue apartment, Edith invited all the staff back with them for a last drink. Luckily Irene, who recognised trouble when she saw it, left the wrong address.

When Edith found out she was absolutely furious. 'You had no right to do that! You bitch!'

She ended up by going to bed and becoming completely delirious. She screamed and shouted. She scratched Irene's face until it bled and, in her anger, she tore her nightdress.

Irene was panic-stricken and contacted Loulou Barrier, who immediately called a doctor.

Edith had to be given a sedative.

Marcel, December 1947, Casablanca

Marcel hadn't boxed for a month. In Casablanca he became the Marcellino of his childhood once again, not bothering about ties or fancy manners. He was his own natural self. On his return from America he threw himself into family life, devoting himself to his sons: Marcel, the oldest, the younger one, René, and little Paul, born in the autumn when he was on the other side of the ocean.

And he spent time with Marinette, his wife. She was still a bit worried about the after-effects of his fight. She didn't think Cerdan looked well and advised him to see a doctor. Cerdan refused. He was convinced that quacks brought him bad luck. He was quite serious when he told Marinette: 'I'd rather not. I'd prefer to take on Raadik again than see a doctor. He might find I have TB.'

Marinette left it at that. Marcel was terribly attentive towards her. He would never tire of Marinette. From the moment he first set eyes on her, he had been bowled over by this pretty blonde with a regular oval face, dainty features and slender figure. Her parents were pork butchers in Mers-Sultan, the chic part of town. Every Sunday she used to watch her brother Narcisse play football. By then, Narcisse Lopez had already acquired a name for himself. He had a good reputation as a player, and a few mentions as a possible for the Moroccan team.

Marinette was proud of him. She washed his kit and sewed the buttons back on his football jersey, as a way of sharing in her elder brother's glory. One Sunday in the Philip Stadium, the Racing Club of Morocco – for whom Narcisse was centre forward – were playing the Banque Union Sport. Cerdan was right wing. It was a Morocco Cup game which promised to be an exciting match. When the teams were presented Cerdan caused a sensation. He was Casablanca's honoured son and France's pride and joy. He was really somebody. The girls flocked round him – he had quite a following – but Marinette only had eyes for her hero Narcisse, not knowing that Cerdan was her brother's hero.

Then the hand of fate intervened, bringing Marcel and Narcisse together. The ball was in the centre of the field and Racing's centre forward seemed to have it under control. Narcisse made it look so easy. He got away from one opponent, then two, then three. He dribbled back and forth, obviously enjoying himself, and revelling in the applause. With a name like Narcisse Lopez you were a star in Casablanca. But then Marcel moved in. Marinette closed her eyes and it was just as well. Nothing could stop Cerdan now. He ran up to Narcisse with loose, powerful strides, and stole the ball from him by barging into him. The referee stared at the tips of his shoes, pretending not to have seen anything. Narcisse was stupefied, Marinette furious. But it was too late. Cerdan made for the other end of the field and scored the winning goal for his team. He had won the heart of the crowd. There were loud cheers for Marcel.

Narcisse didn't hold it against him and introduced his opponent and friend to Marinette that evening. She was seventeen and he twenty-seven. He was just getting over an unhappy love affair and began by treating her like a little girl. But he and Narcisse kept meeting up in Casa-

70

blanca's dusty football fields and he became a frequent visitor at the Lopez home. In the end he couldn't help but notice her: Marinette was turning into a woman. Her looks had already prompted a prison guard to buy her a ring. Marcel was more straightforward. One day he simply asked her: 'Marinette, what are you doing this evening?'

'Nothing. Why, Marcel?'

'Well, we could go to the cinema.'

They went to the cinema. . . And in time they had three children, having got married in between. But first Marcel had had to fight it out with Marinette's parents. Marinette nostalgically recalls the heartwarming story*:

'Who should Marcel and I meet when we came out of the cinema that Sunday, but my father. What bad luck! He pretended not to see us, but when he got home he told my mother off for not supervising me properly.

' "I met Marinette coming out of the Vox with Marcel," he said, trying to sound casual but barely managing to hide his displeasure.

' "With the boxer? *Madre mia*!"

'At supper time when Narcisse and Marcel arrived, there was the most awful scene. My mother went straight for Marcel, brandishing the iron in her hand.

"Be careful what you do to my daughter! A boxer you may be, but if you don't show respect I'll make sure you never forget it."

'Marcel seemed very calm. He burst out laughing and said: "Calm down, calm down. I'll marry your daughter."

* *Cerdan, Marinette Cerdan and René Cerdan*, Solar, Sports 2000.

   ' "You want to marry her? And how are you going to feed her?"

   ' "But Madame Lopez, I'm a boxer."

   ' "Boxer! You call that a career?" '

It was a brief and violent exchange, which brought out all the old arguments between Casablanca's good society and the outcasts in the Marif.

Marcel's background and that of the whole Cerdan clan could be summed up in the word Marif. This was where his father had come a cropper twenty years earlier. He had abandoned his modest butcher's shop in Sidi-Bel-Abbès to set up a café-dancehall in Casablanca, North Africa's oasis on the Atlantic. He had hoped to make his fortune, but it never happened. . .

At home Marcel's mother, three brothers and his sister sometimes didn't have enough to eat. But when the Spanish fishermen who were the majority of their few customers gave them something to fry up, they would have a feast. And although the kids rarely had enough to eat in Casablanca, there was plenty to distract them. In Casablanca – and particularly the quarter called Ferme Blanche, where the Café Cerdan was located, not far from the old medina – you had the ocean, the rocks and, above all, the horse-drawn cabs that the Spanish cab-drivers left there in the evening. They hid in the carriages; the wheels made a sort of maze. But woe betide anyone who got caught!

Marcel and his friends – shoe-shine boys and news-paper-sellers – were fascinated by the way the fishermen on the Corniche Beach mended their black nets before setting out to catch a shoal of sardines.

Papa Cerdan had one passion: boxing. He had a rough manner and spoke quickly in a loud, harsh voice which was husky and often sounded angry. He was always busy, although the customers were few and far between. He held court behind the counter, and a pair of boxing gloves and a skipping-rope hung down between the red, white and blue Chinese lanterns which were lit for the Saturday evening dance.

Conversation at meals in the Cerdan home revolved around hooks, uppercuts and jabs. 'Marcellino' kept his mouth shut. Only his father and brothers spoke. Vincent, the oldest, was the star of the family. He had been to Paris and had got his name in the papers. He had won some important fights against such opponents as the Belgian Scilly, and Maurice Holtzer.

On Saturday afternoons Marcel's father would set up a ring in the dancehall for bouts between members of his family: Vincent, Antoine and Armand to begin with and, later on, Marcel.

At first, 'Marcellino' had to have his ear twisted to make him join in. He preferred playing football in the Turpin Stadium with his friends. But his father would have none of it. Marcel had been forced to put on gloves at the age of nine. Monsieur Cerdan's sons would box or answer to him, by God!

That was how Marcellino learned to fight. At first he practised on his brothers, or a sand-bag, but once he was twelve and weighed 7 stone, he had his first real opponent: the son of Monsieur Delpierre, the announcer at the Majestic Cinema. Even in those early days the fight didn't last long. In the heat of the fight, young Cerdan stuck his thumb into Delpierre Junior's eye. Declared beaten, the latter started sobbing. He was given a bar of chocolate to console him while the victor, Cerdan, was given a beautiful pair of espadrilles. Whereupon Marcellino started stamping his feet and crying.

"What's the matter, Marcel?'

'It's the chocolate, Daddy, I want the chocolate.'

From then onwards, Cerdan's father automatically included Marcel in the programme for all the Thursday meetings he organised in the Oriental Cinema in the rue Hôpital Indigène. And then came Cerdan's real début as a boxer. He was seventeen. It was in June 1933, in Casablanca, of course, in a small room in the Place des Alliés, next to the Saint-Michel service station. Marcellino defeated Gomez on points. Cerdan's father pocketed the prize of 200 francs and a watch. It was just the first of a long and glorious series of punches and wins. A legend was in the making!

Marinette had never watched Marcel fight, not even the previous spring. It would have been a perfect opportunity: Marcel had sent her over to New York with their two sons, Marcel Junior and René, on board the *Queen Elizabeth*. She was pregnant with Paul at the time. He was to fight Harold Green (whom he demolished in 5 minutes 29 seconds) on the 28 March in Madison Square Garden. Cerdan, Marinette, the two children, Lucien Roupp and his wife all moved into Luis Indaco's villa on Long Island. Marinette always had happy memories of this holiday. She would never forget the pretty green cottage with its white windows, on a shady, peaceful drive. Marcel always seemed to be playing boules. She had even taken part herself, to the obvious amazement of her neighbours. The first time Marcel threw the jack, an observant passer-by, thinking that the little block of wood had slipped out of his hands, went to the lengths of bending down to pick it up. Marinette also remembered how well stocked the grocers were. She was thrilled to discover they sold all the fruits they had back home in North Africa.

Marcel was in fantastic shape at that time . . . Now he was exhausted and disenchanted after his fight against Raadik, and she didn't feel like encouraging him to put his gloves on again. The world championship could go hang!

They had talked about everything else but that for the past month. They had discussed the investment of money. She had made him understand the need to save his winnings. He had three children now and had to think of their future. It was very kind of him to give his older brothers Armand and Antoine a Pontiac and a Dodge, but the time had come to start thinking about himself and his family.

Marcel was tired of boxing. He did start training again out of a sense of duty, but he had lost all his self-confidence.

Lucien Roupp bombarded him with telegrams from New York. Marcel knew his manager was fighting with the American organisers to arrange the world championship he had been promised. He knew Roupp and Lew Burston were struggling to get Mr Greene, the President of the National Boxing Association, to give the go-ahead. He knew he was considered the number one challenger to Rocky Graziano (the title-holder), but the boxing world in New York was in a mess – politics! One day it was to be Graziano, the next Tony Zale, and the day after that people were talking about a return fight against Raadik.

Roupp's telegrams were full of conflicting information and urgent requests: 'Send news quickly. Come back. Expecting you in New York.'

But Marcel left Roupp to spend Christmas and the New Year holiday alone in New York with his Christmas tree for company. Why? Because he was only too well aware that America was not the place for him to regain his confidence: every fight there was a tough one. He told the Moroccan correspondent of *But et Club*:

'When I'm in the ring, it's not my manager who

75

suffers, it's me. I'm not a kid any longer. And I have enough experience to be able to arrange my own programme, which will include boxing in Paris. I'm sure that will restore my confidence. I've cabled my plans to Jo Longman asking him to organise a fight in Paris. When Roupp got wind of this, I knew he disapproved. But I warned him that I wouldn't be going back to America until I had fought a European.'

Cerdan had his way. Roupp gave in and Jo Longman organised a European championship specially for Cerdan. His opponent was to be the Italian Manca, and the fight was to take place on 26 January in the Palais des Sports in Paris. The fight was to take the form of a two-round exhibition bout.

Two weeks later, he fought Yanek Walczak, son of Polish emigrants and a well-known and successful fighter at the 'Vel d'Hiv' boxing evenings. He was courageous, decent and likeable. His name, Walczak, meant 'fighter' in Polish. It described him to a T. He went straight in, delivered a few good left jabs, sometimes followed immediately with a right, then ended up with one knee on the ground and his right fist over his stomach doubled up in agony. He heard the referee counting the seconds. Ten seconds went by. There were shouts that it was rigged, but it wasn't. Walczak couldn't stand up.

This time the commentators were full of praise for Marcel's performance. It was patently obvious that his left hook was as fast as ever and he could pack as strong a punch as before. Roupp seized the opportunity that very evening and reminded Marcel about his engagements: 'Marcel, you must go back to America.'

Three weeks earlier, when he was about to set off for France to come and help in Cerdan's corner, Roupp had taken the precaution of signing a contract committing

Cerdan to fight the Texan Lavern Roach, the following March in New York.

That was where Edith was . . .

7

Heartache

Edith, January 1948, New York
She was sitting in her dressing-room at the Versailles, already dressed, her face made up and her hair done. She was surrounded by her bits and pieces: a glass, nose-drops, handkerchief, aspirins, make-up remover pads, notebook and English primer.

Around ten o'clock the manager of the Versailles told the audience: 'Mademoiselle Edith Piaf will be here in five minutes.' The manager made a sign to Pancho, the conductor. The musicians stopped playing their noisy sambas and there was complete silence when Edith appeared on the raised podium.

Edith, wearing her long-sleeved black dress, had been singing here for just under an hour every evening since 14 January.

She finished each of her songs with a characteristic gesture. Accompanied by Robert Chauvigny on the piano and Marc Bonel on the accordion, and backed by a chorus concealed behind a big curtain, Edith began with '*Le pirate*' from the film *Etoile sans Lumière*, which she made in 1945 with Yves Montand and Serge Reggiani. She ended with '*La vie en rose.*'

This was by far the audience's favourite song. And Edith put more into it than into any of the others. The song was now four years old. It went back to the christening of Piaf's little god-daughter, Jeanine, daughter of the composer Louiguy. There were about fifteen of them at table in her house in the rue Anatole-de-la-Forge, near the Etoile. When the meal was over a radiant Edith took Louis Barrier away to a back room where there was a piano. Louiguy tinkled out a few notes. All of a sudden Piaf cried out, '*Je vois la vie en rose*' ('Life is great'). The song started out as a flash of inspiration, but it was left to languish at the bottom of a drawer because it had no story to it. Later on, Piaf gave '*La vie en rose*' to Marianne Michel, but it was Piaf herself who eventually brought it to life and made it a success:

> '*Quand il me prend dans ses bras,*
> *Il me parle tout bas,*
> *Je vois la vie en rose,*
> *Il me dit des mots d'amour,*
> *Des mots de tous les jours*
> *Et ça m'fait quelque chose . . .*'

('When he takes me in his arms/And whispers softly to me/Life is great/He talks of love/Sweet nothings/And it goes to my head . . .')

Piaf was asked for an encore every evening. And she was only too delighted to sing this song a second time. Robert, Provys and Fischer had been right to gamble on her name. This time she had the audiences eating out of her hand. In his column in the *New York Herald Tribune*, Bert McCord likened her to an actress rather than a singer.

It was in the rococo décor of the Versailles with its pink and white plaster, statues, miniature trees, mirrors, windows, heavy drapes and crystal chandeliers that *la môme* Piaf tamed America.

Her other old favourite was '*L'accordéoniste*'. It was

about an accordionist 'who can play the "java".' The song was conceived by Michel Emer at the beginning of 1940. He was wounded in the war and was convalescing in the Lakanal High School in Sceaux, which had been turned into a military hospital. The song came to him one night in a dream. He wrote it down the next day and contacted Piaf.

At first she put him off politely. 'Listen, I'm very busy at the moment, call me again in two months.'

Emer was insistent. 'But I'm going back to the front.'

'Well, come and see me this evening at six then.'

Piaf was white as a sheet when Emer, ill at ease in his uniform, struck the last note on the piano. 'Play it again,' she said. He played it more than ten times and was still tinkling away on the piano at six in the morning.

Searching for some sign of approval on her part he kept asking for reassurance: 'Do you like it, Madame Edith?'

'Of course I do. I like it so much that I'm going to sing it in two days' time.'

Edith had given her word. And Michel Emer's words and music struck a chord in the hearts of the audience in the Amiral, the night-club on the rue Arsène Houssaye, near the Etoile.

Edith and Michel then became friends. Piaf valued Emer's talent at composing words and music at the same time and the way his tunes caught on immediately, almost as though people were already going round singing them.

And then who should turn up at the Versailles, almost straight from the boat, but Emer. He had come to New York to work on some new musical arrangements. Edith was naturally his first port of call. He entered her dressing-room as she was about to go on stage.

She was bubbling over with excitement: 'Hi there, little soldier. I hope you've brought me a song.'

'No, I've come to say hello,' said Emer, taken aback.

'Well, listen. We'll say hello when you've written me a song. Off you go, now!'

Emer didn't watch Piaf's performance. He stayed behind in her dressing-room and wrote *'Bal dans ma rue'*. He had earned his kiss. Piaf gave him a big one on the cheek.

Emer, who was on top form, gave in to another of Edith's demands the next day in the Park Avenue apartment.

'The song you wrote yesterday was very nice. I'll sing it to you. But I need another where someone dies at the end.'

Unruffled, Emer replied: 'Why not? Someone can always get killed.'

Michel Emer's visit and creative inspiration provided a huge boost to Edith's morale. She confided in her friend from Paris: 'You see, the Yanks are getting to know me. And they are keen to know me better. . .'

She never spoke a truer word. There was a stream of Broadway stars at the Versailles. Marlene Dietrich was full of praise, and the publicity did Edith nothing but good. They soon became friends.

One evening after her performance, Gene Kelly and John Garfield came to offer her their effusive congratulations. When she got back to the apartment at one in the morning she told Irene the big news. Edith had met a guy – and what a guy! – with the most amazing physique she had ever seen. And he was coming to dinner the following evening and was to be given three-star treatment.

It was John Garfield. Irene didn't try to argue. She knew Garfield by name and reputation and had seen him in his last few films. She was delighted to meet him, but she knew what was going to happen.

Garfield and Piaf had too much in common. To start

with, they had both been brought up on the streets. He was born in a cheerless part of New York, the Lower East Side. His family had moved up a rung to a slum in Brooklyn and then settled in the Bronx. His father, a humble Jewish tailor, had the greatest difficulty in making ends meet. Left to his own devices in an environment where juvenile delinquency was common, it wasn't long before John Garfield got into trouble. His father was at the end of his tether and had him put in a reformatory for young hooligans. When he came out, Garfield drifted into theatre and cinema. The only roles he got were gangsters or baddies.

Piaf fell in love not only with Garfield's virile physique but with his true-life rags-to-riches story, about which he was quite open. It was just like an American-style thriller with all its violence and squalor. It was no accident that, after twenty violent films, John should finally become famous in *The Postman Always Rings Twice*, a film based on the novel by James M. Cain, which had been rejected by Metro-Goldwyn-Mayer as too 'hot' and then shelved for twelve years.

John came back to 891 Park Avenue every evening. A pattern was established. A taxi would pick up Edith at 9.30 p.m. on the dot. Irene would stay behind and make conversation with John until Edith returned.

Married with two children, John wouldn't allow himself to be seen in public with Edith. He didn't want any trouble. Irene noticed an expression of well-being on Piaf's face in the morning. Edith kept telling her, 'I can't believe how kind he is, this guy.'

Was it true love? It was always true love with Piaf. As if there were anything else . . .

When Garfield had to leave Edith to finish shooting *Force of Evil* in Hollywood, Edith decided she had to see him again as soon as possible. The Versailles was closed that evening. New York was blanketed in snow. It was banked up against the skyscrapers. There was no traffic – no buses, no taxis. But Edith had decided they must go out, come what may. An old-fashioned cinema on 42nd Street was showing an old Garfield film. What an opportunity! Irene's hesitation was overruled; they would both make their way through the snow to 42nd Street!

The seats cost 50 cents but Edith would have paid the earth. She was spellbound. Every time Garfield came on she pinched Irene's arm and pestered her: 'Isn't he handsome? Look how handsome he is!'

The words *The End* appeared all too soon for Edith. Now they had to go all the way back to 78th Street. But they had nothing to look forward to this time. Their return to the apartment was a frightening experience.

A few weeks later, Garfield invited both of them to a big party at his home. It was a very formal reception with the cream of New York society and a sprinkling of Hollywood stars. And it provided an opportunity to introduce Madame Piaf, with all due deference and in the most charming manner, to Roberta Mann, the mother of John Garfield's children. It was an elegant way of drawing a curtain over the episode.

Edith and Marcel, 12 March 1948, New York, Madison Square Garden

Edith, looking radiant in a fur coat, was in a ringside seat in Madison Square Garden. Jean-Louis Jaubert was on her right looking very smart, as usual. Both had come to the end of their American contracts. Edith's last show at the Versailles had been on 10 March, two days earlier. Edith had celebrated her reunion with the Compagnons, just back from Florida and Chicago, in her Park Avenue apartment. Their friendship had been a bit strained when they had said goodbye at the beginning of December. Since then, Edith's success at the Versailles had erased the memory of her semi-failure at the Playhouse. She had her companions back. They promised each other they would go on tour again together.

But Cerdan was the one who dominated her evening. Theirs had been an even longer separation and she was overjoyed when she saw him again, while he was bursting with the energy of an athlete on peak form.

It was hard to associate the man who had beaten Georgie Abrams, Harold Green, Billy Walker and Anton Raadik with this thin chap who had come to fight Lavern Roach. His features were firm, and so were his muscles; his waist was slim, his eyes alert and his chin up. He had arrived from Paris on 27 February with Lucien Roupp and Jo Longman. He was already in good shape. They kept a closer eye on him during the two weeks of training in the US than ever before. The memory of the fight against Raadik was still fresh in their minds.

'Do you know, they even tried to keep me under lock and key, they watched me so closely,' confided Marcel to Edith. She burst out laughing.

Ten days or so before Marcel returned to America, Irene de Trébert had left the apartment on Park Avenue and gone back to Paris for a show.

Edith wanted to see Cerdan immediately. Far from trying to get out of it, he jumped at the opportunity of paying her a visit. It was lucky that the dates coincided. Edith finished at the Versailles as he was preparing to enter the ring at Madison Square Garden. It seemed as though the two of them were destined to meet up – and they didn't attempt to fight against destiny.

It was the first time Edith had watched Marcel box. It would never have occurred to her to spend an evening at Madison Square Garden. But her admiration for the boxer

84

was growing and she was enchanted by the idea of seeing him perform in the ring.

She didn't ask him anything about his opponent; what could she have asked him anyway? He volunteered the information. He told her that Lavern Roach was a young man whom the Americans seemed to hold in high esteem and that he (Cerdan) would have to watch out. A defeat would destroy all his hopes of getting a crack at the world championship.

Marcel was right. He sensed that the American public and media might well give him a hard time in this final 'qualifying exam'. It was almost a year to the day since Marcel had last fought in New York. Did this explain why Cerdan was no longer so highly rated? The last time he had fought there against Harold Green, the new Yorkers had been so sympathetic towards him. Now they seemed to be rooting against him and in favour of Lavern Roach. But the Texan's track record was nothing to write home about and he hardly justified such enthusiasm.

Slumped in her seat, Piaf guessed that Marcel was not only going to have his opponent to deal with, but also a hostile audience. What she didn't know was that Cerdan faced an additional handicap in the shape of Donovan, who was responsible for giving the final decision. When Lucien Roupp learned that Donovan had been chosen as referee from amongst seven or eight candidates, he was upset, 'Oh no, not him!'

An American friend, who practically lived in Madison Square Garden, had warned him quite seriously that people were scheming against Marcel and that Donovan should be avoided at all costs. Roupp immediately went to see Colonel Eagan, the great New York State boxing baron, to express his concern about Donovan's impartiality.

Eagan was blandly reassuring: 'Don't worry. I'll look

after it. I appoint the referees at the last minute at the ringside. I won't nominate Donovan.'

Roupp deliberately said nothing to Cerdan in order not to disrupt his preparation or undermine his morale and quiet confidence. Marcel was very flattered to find Mike Jacobs, the patriarch of New York boxing, at the ringside that evening. Once again he had interrupted his period of convalescence in Florida for Cerdan. Roupp and Cerdan felt that having this wise old man here provided the best guarantee possible of a clean fight.

But Roupp had been taken in. He was stunned to see Donovan stepping over the rope just after he had taken up position in Marcel's corner. So much for Eagan's word! Roupp then told Cerdan to get it all over as quickly as possible. Knowing Cerdan, who was already completely caught up in the fight, he was short and sharp. 'Listen, Marcel, you've got to be quick! And I mean quick!'

And Marcel plunged in. He landed a right hook on Lavern Roach's jaw in the second round. The Texan bent double and collapsed on the floor. Donovan counted to nine. Roach got up and fell over again. And Donovan started counting again from one! And so it went on. How long was Roach on the mat in all? Nat Fleischer, the editor of *Ring* magazine who kept his hand on his stop-watch, was able to give a quick answer: 32 seconds! It was a record unequalled in boxing history. The previous record of this nature, sadly famous, went back to the 1920s. Gene Tunney had spent 14 seconds on the mat and, strengthened by this extended 'knock-down', had come back to beat Jack Dempsey!

This incident, which shook the Garden and gave Marcel back 'his' audience, threw Cerdan. He got worked up like a beginner. Many of his punches failed to connect. His second wind was a long time coming. And he was completely shattered between the fourth and seventh rounds.

Then came the decisive round. Marcel delivered a left hook which floored Lavern Roach for the third time. The Texan got up on the count of two, but this time Donovan stopped the fight. Roach had taken enough punishment and wouldn't go on.

Significantly, Colonel Eagan, who had made a point of congratulating Marcel after his previous fights, didn't show up in Cerdan's dressing-room.

Robert Bré wrote the following acid commentary in *But et Club*:

> 'Thank God Marcel managed to calm down! He was in good shape and proved that he could stay in there for more than five rounds. The Americans will have to try a different approach. And they will. But, given Marcel's state of mind at the moment, I don't think they'll be any luckier. Cerdan has his sights set on the world crown. He has it in for certain US boxing personalities. I feel sorry for the next American boxer they serve up to him. As I feel sorry for Lavern Roach, the only true victim of this affair. Poor Roach was sacrificed for a cause which had nothing to do with sport.'

Robert Bré sought Edith Piaf's opinion as a matter of course. He knew her well. He was the only one of the French press correspondents in New York to be able to count himself in her circle. He had gone to meet her off the boat when she had arrived last October. He followed her to the Playhouse and then the Versailles. He also knew the apartment at 891 Park Avenue. He and Maurice Chevalier had been only too delighted to show Edith and Irene de Trébert round New York.

'Well, Edith, what do you think?' Robert Bré asked her.

Edith was still reeling from the shock, and the magic, of the fight. 'You would never guess,' she replied. 'I've experienced all sorts of different emotions in my time but nothing's hit me this hard. It's quite something to see a little chap from back home, lost amongst thousands of Yankees, all alone in the ring, defending our name.'

'Weren't you worried for Marcel?'

'Not for a second! I was numb. But when Marcel knocked the other chap on to the floor with that amazing punch, I didn't feel too good at all.'

'Do you like boxing now?'

'I used to hate it. But since watching Marcel. . . I've changed my mind. He makes it look beautiful. And I'm proud. This guy really has guts. To think I was actually shouting, "Go on Marcel, kill him." It's crazy. And no one could make me shut up.'

Robert Bré put his notes together and on Tuesday 16 March there was a surprising article by Piaf on page 2 of *Paris Presse* under the heading, 'Thank you, Marcel. You're great.'

Edith and Marcel read it together when they got back to Paris. They were the only people who understood what Edith meant when she said, 'Now I'm sure I've got it bad.'

8

'Piaf Jinx on Cerdan'

'Mummy, mummy, he's not playing fair.' Michel Legrand, aged five, clung to his mother, Irene de Trébert, seeking refuge from this man who didn't box by the rules.

Marcel went pink with embarrassment and tried to apologise but Irene saw the funny side and burst out laughing: 'That will teach you, Michel. You don't know who this man is, do you?'

Edith then broke in and, radiating happiness, put her hand on little Michel's shoulder, saying: 'You know, Marcel is stronger than Tarzan and Zorro put together.'

Irene de Trébert had insisted on inviting Edith and Marcel to lunch on their arrival from New York. She went to meet them at Orly. It was drizzling. Because of strong westerly winds, the plane had landed an hour early. Piaf and Cerdan had made no attempt to avoid the cameras when they reached the foot of the gangway. The photos went the rounds of all the newspaper offices and people thought it was a coincidence that these two great French stars, flushed with victory, their arms full of flowers, should make a triumphant return together.

The pilots had presented Edith with two bouquets of brightly coloured tulips which she kissed before giving one to Marcel. Marcel was in high spirits. The reigning Miss Cotton, who was also on board, got caught up in the general mood, burst out laughing and, in her exuberance, posed on Marcel's arm. She hadn't been expecting such a welcome in Paris.

Edith was radiant with happiness. She sang 'Y'a pas d'printemps'. And Marcel couldn't stop laughing.

Irene had been careful not to tell people about the relationship between Edith and Marcel whose beginnings she had witnessed five months earlier in New York. She had no idea why or how it had sprung to life again. It was a long time before she got used to Cerdan being in Piaf's circle. There were more surprises in store for her.

Four days later, on Friday 19 March, Irene had the pleasure of accompanying Edith and Marcel to a special gala at the Théâtre du Club des Cinq under the sponsorship of François Mitterand, no less, *Ministre des Anciens Combattants* (Minister for Veterans' Affairs), and Pierre de Gaulle, *President du Conseil Municipal* (President of the Municipal Council).

Piaf, Pierre Dac and Irene Hilda had graciously agreed to provide their support and the poster announced that Cerdan would be introduced to the public during the evening. The seats were 800 francs each. The Club des Cinq was more crowded than ever.

After the show, Emile, Edith's chauffeur, came by to take them both to Montmartre. Edith had grown tired of the Claridge and had moved into 7 rue Leconte de Lisle, a quiet street in a peaceful, smart neighbourhood, a stone's thrown from the Eglise d'Auteuil. It had a wooden front door. On the ground floor there was a small corridor, with a kitchen on the left and a big living-room on the right. On the first floor there were three bedrooms, a bathroom and a small study which served as a bedroom for Ginou and Solange, the maid, who was a bright, exuberant young Eurasian. It was the first time in her life Edith had really felt as though a place was hers.

Edith told Simone Berteaut, 'Momone': 'When someone

like Cerdan comes into your life, the least you can do is offer him a home.'

Edith and Marcel were now living together in Paris. To begin with Marcel had tried to divide his time between the rue d'Orsel and the rue Leconte de Lisle in order not to hurt Paul Genser's feelings and spoil their friendship. Genser was very possessive about Marcel. Poor Paul was disheartened when Marcel turned up one evening in a suit and tie with the self-absorbed look of someone who has resolved to make a complete break with the past.

'Paul, don't be angry with me. I must go.'

'Really, where to?' Paul couldn't understand it. He tried to get Marcel to look at him, but he kept evading his glance. Marcel started getting his things together. Paul pressed him: 'Must you really go? Aren't you all right here?'

'I can't explain, Paul. You know that has nothing to do with it.'

Paul was on the verge of tears when Marcel left. He had to pull himself together. After all, Marcel must have a good reason for leaving. But he thought he should tell Lucien Roupp what had happened.

'What's up with Marcel?'

Roupp understood the situation. He tried to reassure Paul. 'Let him live his own life, Paul. He's not himself at the moment. There's someone . . . He'll get over it . . .'

This was the first Paul knew of the affair between Piaf and Cerdan. At first he refused to believe it. Marcel was undoubtedly making a big mistake. Roupp would have been the first to agree.

One morning in the rue Leconte de Lisle, Piaf picked up the phone and called Jacques Bourgeat. 'Jacques, there's someone I must introduce you to. Can you come over?'

That afternoon, Solange opened the door to a big man

with a fresh complexion, grey hair and broad shoulders, dressed in an English overcoat in a bold herring-bone design.

Edith had told Marcel in advance: 'You're going to meet a marvellous man. A man to whom I owe everything.' Edith could talk about nothing but Jacques. Marcel laughed when she said: 'Let me tell you straight away that he's neither my father nor a boyfriend.'

'So who is he then, Edith?' Marcel asked.

'He's my mentor.'

His eyes opened in astonishment. Edith went on, going back into the past. 'I met him in 1935, more than ten years ago. He immediately became my guide. How can I explain it to you? I didn't know anything about anything. One day he took me to the Louvre, then the next Sunday we went to the Orangerie. He gave me books to read. You can't imagine what a pain it was at the beginning. But when you've read then you feel so much better. It makes you feel good inside.'

Marcel was full of awe when he shook hands with Jacques Bourgeat. Bourgeat put him at his ease. They talked about boxing, the cinema, America. Marcel hadn't been expecting anything like this from an intellectual who, according to Edith, knew all there was to know about everything.

Jacques Bourgeat refused to form an opinion about Cerdan on this first meeting. He had enough tact and psychological insight not to make any superficial judgments.

Bourgeat was working at the Bibliothèque Nationale (National Library) where he was later to become the curator. He was a poet and philosopher. He had written a pleasing anthology of poems, *'Au petit trot de Pégase'*, and Edith's first song *'Chant d'habit'*. He managed to make her learn Plato's *Symposium* by heart. They tackled the

92

Apology on another occasion. Bourgeat had read it through slowly, making very simple comments on the text. When he came to the end, after Socrates had told those round him, 'The time has now come for us to go our separate ways: you to live and I to die . . .' Piaf held her breath; tears were flowing down her cheeks.

Later, when Edith had become a star, she gave him the first photo she had taken at Harcourt's as a celebrated artiste. She dedicated it: '*A mon Jacquot, amitiés esternelles*' ('To Jacquot, in eternal friendship'). Bourgeat couldn't stop laughing and told her that she had unconsciously imitated the mediaeval writers (the normal spelling being *éternelles*). She took it as a compliment. Edith blossomed at Bourgeat's Sunday school.

Marcel began training again for his match against Lucien Krawsyck set for 25 March in the 'Vel d'Hiv'. Edith was starting a one-month run at the Théâtre des Ambassadeurs that evening. Life in the rue Leconte de Lisle was organised round this double fixture. Marcel hid himself away to avoid gossip and elude the press photographs. Whenever they went out he laid himself down on the back seat of the car. Edith got a great kick out of seeing Marcel play hide-and-seek. But Marcel didn't seem to enjoy it. He was a bit irritated at having to live this clandestine existence. And he was told not to answer the bell when Edith was out.

Marcel made sure he didn't go to bed too late. He ran in the Bois de Boulogne every morning and went to the gym in the late afternoon for a few practice rounds. Their schedules didn't quite coincide. Marcel made a big effort in the evenings and struggled with his tiredness to provide moral support while she rehearsed.

After dinner, the Piaf clique would move to the sitting-room and gather round Marguerite Monnot at the piano. Edith called her 'Ma Guitte'. She had met her before the war in Le Gerny's, a club in the rue Pierre Charron, opposite the Belle Ferronnière. With her straight ash-blonde hair and pale complexion often without make-up, she had a noble profile, a face from the Middle Ages.

Marcel liked her because she was discreet and because she pampered Edith and was forever calling her 'my pet'. She was the only woman who crossed Edith's path without leaving in a storm of acrimony. In fact, she herself was permanently in the clouds. So dreamy was La Guitte that you felt she needed someone to look after her.

With her fingers intertwined and her elbows on the varnished wood of the piano, Edith let herself be carried away by Marguerite Monnot's music. Marcel would bow out when Edith became Piaf again. He would go upstairs to bed, blowing kisses from afar. The only time they really had to themselves was at the beginning of the afternoon. Edith noticed that Marcel had children's books and comics in his case: Pim-Pam-Poum, Buffalo Bill, Nick Carter, Tom Mix. . . It made her laugh. She loved it when Marcel retold his heroes' adventures, in his own ingenuous fashion. As a child, Marcel had only attended school for five years.

'Yes, but,' he told Edith, 'I won a prize. A history prize. I adored Bayard and Du Guesclin.'

Edith was overcome with tenderness. 'I understand, darling.'

'Do you realise,' he said, 'those guys used to take on ten or fifteen men single-handed. They really knew how to fight.'

Marcel told Edith the story of the heroic battle at Garigliano Bridge. That was all he could remember. As for the rest . . . Botany, zoology, geology and anatomy, which were all incomprehensible to him, had made less of an impression on Marcel than a teacher with only one arm who used to hit his pupils with his one good hand. This was another story that moved Edith.

'He taught the second year and I was in the first. His empty sleeve terrified me. I used to tell myself, next year, it'll be your turn, Marcel. . . .'

Edith closed her eyes.

'You can't imagine what it was like,' Marcel went on. 'It kept me awake at night. Eventually I realised the only solution was to jump the next class. I've never worked so hard in my life.' It was the first time Marcel had boasted in front of Edith.

She burst out laughing. 'Don't imagine I've got a baccalauréat.'

He replied, 'But you know about a lot of things.'

She shrugged her shoulders: 'I shouldn't make a song and dance about it. Just do what I do, read the books you need to read.'

That was how he found himself reading an amazing book: *Keys of the Kingdom* by A. J. Cronin. This, his first book, became symbolic. Marcel took it everywhere. For him it was a sort of miracle-book, the key to a new world of learning.

But the day came when he had to trade in Cronin for Krawsyck. It was a fight that Lucien Roupp would have preferred to avoid. It didn't add up to anything on paper or in the ring, except for the promoters whose primary aim had been to make money, and who did so. Fighting an opponent whose one concern was to protect himself, all Cerdan's efforts were wasted. It took him ten rounds to finish off Krawsyck. He won on points which only added a rather flat victory to his record.

He was cornered by the press. Convinced that he hadn't really got into the fight, he made no effort to contradict the critics.

'How did the fight go, sir?'

95

'I couldn't do anything, Emile. There was no way of getting him to drop his guard.'

Emile, Piaf's chauffeur, couldn't have been more attentive and respectful towards him. Marcel was flattered to be addressed as 'sir'. It had never happened to him before.

Sometimes he would meet up with Edith in her dressing-room at the Ambassadeurs. She and the Compagnons were the best of friends. One evening he had the pleasure of bringing Joe Louis, world heavyweight champion and a hero in world boxing. They dined with Edith and Jo Longman after the show. And Edith introduced Marcel to everyone who was anyone in Paris, when they came to see her in the wings and at her table. Marcel was particularly fond of one of the Compagnons called Jo Frachon, the gentle giant, whose noble and genuine feelings for Edith Marcel recognised.

When Edith felt a sudden desire to be close to God, Jo Frachon would come and pick her up in the rue Leconte de Lisle and take her to the Eglise d'Auteuil. He would ring the doorbell. Solange would welcome him and Edith would hurtle down the stairs. Jo always had something nice to say to her. Edith would put her arm through Jo's as they went out. They made a funny pair, so different were they in height. But it made Marcel feel good to see them. He would lean on the window ledge and cry out to Jo: 'Whatever you do, look after my little one. Bring her back quickly.'

Marcel had changed considerably in the month he had been there. He had become more and more attached to Edith and tried to spend as much time with her as possible. He was dazzled by her.

There were no suitable opponents for him in France so, to keep his hand in, a fight was to be held in Brussels on 23 May. Marcel made the mistake of not taking it very

he day after Marcel's triumph in the ring – the two lovers with their friend Felix Levitan
ACME NEWSPICTURES

Edith and Marcel on the same bill at the Club des Cinq, March 1948
A.F.P.

Edith studying English in her room at the Ambassador Hotel, New York
A.F.P.

Cerdan before his fight against Tony Zale, reading John Steinbeck's *In Dubious Battle*

Cerdan at Loch Sheldrake
KEYSTONE

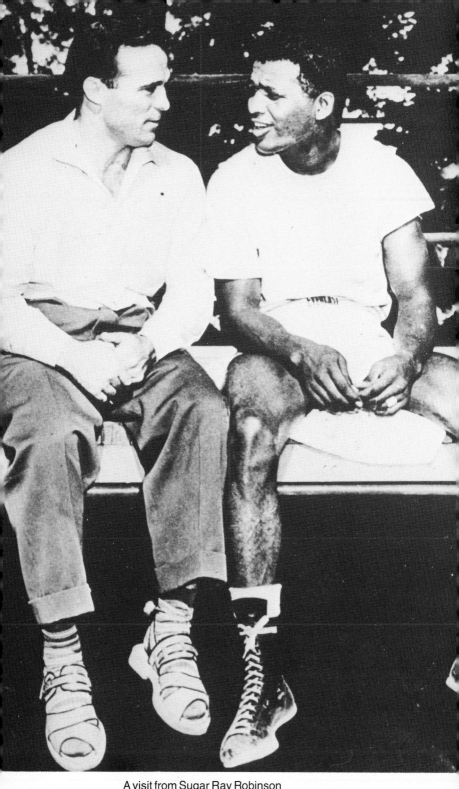

A visit from Sugar Ray Robinson

Tony Zale *(left)* taking a beating from Marcel Cerdan . . .
KEYSTONE

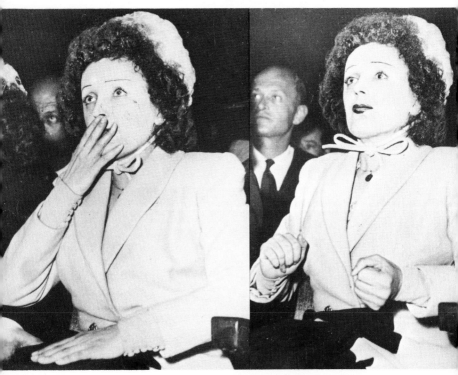

. . . while Edith watches on, her heart in her mouth
FELIX LEVITAN COLLECTION

Congratulations after winning the world championship. Marcel Cerdan with
Lucien Roupp, Fernandel, Jo Longman and Jo Rizzo
KEYSTONE

Edith performing to a full house at the Versailles in New York, October 1948
UPI

Edith and Marcel with Marguerite Monnot, who composed the music for 'A Hymn to Lo

The wreckage of the ill-fated Air France flight that crashed in the Azores on
28 October 1949 killing everyone aboard

seriously. A few days later, Roupp received the contract they had been waiting for. It was for the world championship and it guaranteed that Cerdan would take on the winner of the Zale-Graziano fight for the title. But there was a clause in it which cancelled everything should Marcel lose a fight. Roupp tried in vain to warn his boxer about the dangers of treating the Belgian fight too casually, but Marcel did exactly as he pleased, carried away by his own exuberance. He rushed his training and as soon as it was over, he dashed off to meet Edith in a state of feverish excitement.

Marcel, 23 May 1948, Brussels

Roupp rented a flat in Brussels and Marcel took the opportunity of inviting his brother Antoine to join them. He was lent the garden of a famous bar, the Moder Lambic. Although he had a touch of lumbago and his right hand hurt when he entered the ring, he thought he would be able to polish off his opponent, the Belgian Cyrille Delannoit, fairly quickly. He had thought he was in better shape than he was. It was a disaster from the word go: the English referee, Mr Little, declared Delannoit the winner. Cerdan was destroyed by the decision and collapsed in the ring, sobbing like a child. He was heartbroken as he had nurtured the ambition of retiring unbeaten, which no other boxer in the world, not even Gene Tunney or Joe Louis, had been able to do.

He placed a call to Paris: JAS 22.92 as soon as he got back from the fight. It was Edith's number in the rue Leconte de Lisle. While he was waiting for the call to come through he went upstairs to have a bath. Paris replied. She wasn't in. She had already set off for the ABC where she was appearing in a new show with the Compagnons and Armand Mestral. She had left a message which Solange read out to him: 'Madame said her heart was with you. She took a radio to the ABC and heard the whole broadcast. She is horrified by the result.'

Marcel left his room and they all sat down to eat. There were about twenty of them, including the seconds and their wives. It wasn't a celebratory blow-out, but the dinner was far from gloomy. Marcel had a good appetite; he ate ham, pâté, veal cutlet, chips and rice pudding. As his right hand was swollen, Jacqueline, Jo Longman's girlfriend, cut his meat for him. Towards the end of the meal, Antoine Cerdan, Roupp and Jo withdrew for a council of war. Marcel watched the three of them, particularly Antoine. Marcel knew that as far as Antoine was concerned he would always be the little one in short trousers. Antoine was the only person who dared bawl him out. Sometimes when Antoine was cross with Marcel it was all he could do to stop himself from smacking Marcel.

Marcel didn't sleep a wink all night. He renewed his decision to give up boxing. His reception at the Gare du Nord the next morning was on the cool side. A little boy separated himself from the cynical crowd staring at Cerdan and clutched at his legs: 'Mr Cerdan, you must fight Delannoit again. We all want you to be champion.'

Cerdan ruffled the boy's hair and gave his promise, or pretended to. Paul had come to pick him up and Cerdan quickly disappeared into his car. Paul added his own spontaneous word of comfort: 'Don't do anything silly, Marcel, will you! Remember the world championship. Pull yourself together.'

Cerdan shrugged his shoulders. 'What are you talking about? I'm not even the European champion any longer.'

The subject was closed. Cerdan had decided to give up boxing. But he had reckoned without Edith. She rose to the attack, hands on hips: 'What did you say?'

'No, no, don't go on about it. You were wrong to make

98

me go back on my decision after the fight against Raadik. Now it's over. My future is settled. Let's not talk about it any more.'

'But it's not up to you!'

'What do you mean?'

'No. Don't forget that you, as Cerdan, have a duty to people other than yourself.' She became tender: 'All the people who love you and support you still believe in you. And you want to leave them in the lurch? You're crazy, Marcel!'

Suddenly, everything became clear to Marcel. He understood that she was exerting over him the power she usually brought to bear over her audience. He was spellbound.

In his agitation, he had forgotten one thing: the power of the media. On 30 May, issue number 91 of *France-Dimanche* carried an explosive headline eight columns wide on its front page: 'PIAF JINX ON CERDAN'.

'Bastards!' screamed Edith. It was too much for her to stomach, and he was deeply distressed. It was as though the media had hit him below the belt. He could see Casablanca, Marinette, the kids in his mind's eye. It was awful. 'They'll pay for this,' screamed Edith. She was pale.

They decided to organise a visit *and* issue an invitation to punish these 'bastards' who hadn't actually revealed very much. All they had done was to give a straightforward account of Piaf and Cerdan's meeting in New York.

'Since his return from America in 1947,' wrote *France-Dimanche*, 'Cerdan sees Edith Piaf every day. She goes to all his fights. He goes to hear her sing every evening. Cerdan finds Piaf attractive in the sense that she can talk about music, literature and poetry, all of which is a new universe for Cerdan, who is developing a taste for the pleasures of society.'

It didn't seem enough to warrant talk of jinxes. But more important than the disclosure of their relationship, those words hurt – particularly for people who were haunted by superstition.

A plan was drawn up. Roupp and Longman were to go and beat up the paper's editor and Edith would invite the author of the offending article to her home.

Max Corre, who was then editor of *France-Dimanche* (six foot tall and 14 stone) writes:

'I was working in my office. The *France-Dimanche* offices were on the fifth floor of the *France-Soir* office block on the rue Réaumur. We had a little office which was very easy to get into. They had no difficulty finding it. When Roupp and Longman burst in, it was immediately obvious that they had come on a serious mission. Roupp stayed calm but Longman seemed overwrought. He was fiddling with a big ring that I think he wore on his left hand. They wasted no time. The fight started straight away. Roupp stayed in his corner. He didn't seem too unhappy when Longman got hit. In fact Roupp almost laughed at him. To this day I can hear him say, "Your left, Jo." Other guys from the *France-Dimanche* team rallied round. Longman recognised his limitations. He didn't insist. Eight days later he called me up to tell me he didn't hold it against me, that it had all been sorted out. My hand still hurt. I wasn't experienced; I didn't know how to clench my fist the way boxers do. I broke a finger.'

Georges Cravenne, the prime source for the article, had been a journalist on *Ciné Magazine*, *Paris-Soir*, and *L'Intransigeant*, before becoming a freelance contributor to

100

France-Dimanche. He is now a producer at the Tout-Paris. This is his account:

'I knew Edith Piaf very well. There was nothing I didn't know about her affair with Cerdan. When I was in Brussels reporting on Marcel, I got a phone call from *France-Dimanche*. Cerdan's defeat had gone down badly in Paris. The newspaper now had the opportunity of getting a story out of it. I agreed to send a few notes. I was asked for some information which I was one of the few people to know: Edith's private telephone number in the rue Leconte de Lisle. That's what gave the game away. The article was anonymous, but it included the ultra-confidential number. It didn't take Edith and Marcel long to put two and two together. Marcel called me. He asked me to come to the rue Leconte de Lisle. I knew exactly what to expect but I didn't feel like turning tail. I rang and went in. He was waiting for me in the sitting-room. He was holding the newspaper. Without so much as a hello, he pushed it at me: "You wrote this!"

'I said, "No".

'He said, "But you gave them the telephone number!"

'I said, "Yes".

'That was when I experienced a sort of electric shock. He had punched me. I hadn't even seen it coming. I spun round but didn't fall over and made straight for the door. The whole thing was over in fifteen seconds. I never saw Cerdan again . . .'

Back in Casablanca, Marcel was told that the President of the French Boxing Federation was planning to offer him a retirement position on the pre-Olympic training course

101

for amateur boxers in Uriage, 'far from the city and its temptations'.

It was an ambiguous proposal. It would appear that people were upset by the company Marcel kept in Paris. For the time being, there were only three things that mattered to Marcel: getting his revenge over Delannoit, going back to the farm he had just bought at Sidi Marouf, seven miles from Casablanca, and seeing Edith again, who was fretting in his absence. Finding herself between shows, Edith filled the lonely hours by lovingly knitting pullovers for her boxer.

Edith, June 1948, Paris
One lunchtime, Momone rushed over to the rue Leconte de Lisle. She asked Solange if Edith was still asleep and without waiting for a reply, climbed the stairs two at a time. She sat down on the end of Edith's bed. Edith had something amazing to tell her.

'Momone, what's happening to me? I've never met a man like this before.'

'Marcel?'

'Who else, you nut? You'll never guess what!'

'Has he ditched you?'

Piaf shook her head. 'Nothing like that. But I won't deny that I was scared stiff. Can you imagine – I noticed that Marcel had been leaving the house at the same time every day for three days. So I told myself, "Your little friend is hiding something from you." I started to get tired of it. I wanted to know who he was meeting.'

'You don't mean to say you followed him!'

'That's exactly what I did!'

Momone burst out laughing. 'So what did she look like?'

'Silly cow! I can see you don't know Marcel! I'll tell you who he was with. You should have seen this chap's face, poor thing . . . It was pitiful. And there was Marcel holding on to him like a little dog. I wanted to find out what was going on. I crept up on them. And then Marcel saw me. I pretended to be surprised – "Oh, Marcel!" You can just imagine the scene. Then he introduced me: "Edith, this is my friend Novarro, a childhood friend, a football pal from Casa." '

'And what was it all about?' asked Simone.

'Well, this Novarro was losing his sight; the poor thing was three-quarters blind. When Marcel found out he made him come to Paris immediately. And he'd been taking him to an occulist every day for three days.' Edith sat up in bed, patted her pillows and took a deep breath. 'You see, Momone, chaps like Marcel aren't two a penny, believe me.'

Tony and Rocky, 9 June 1948, New Jersey

It was the third and last fight in the battle between Tony (Zale) and Rocky (Graziano) for the world title. The first fight had been won by Tony on 27 September 1946. Rocky had a rough time of it and fell heavily in the sixth round. He got up in time but the umpire stopped him, to Rocky's fury. 'Whenever you want, wherever you want, and we'll see what happens,' he told Zale. It happened ten months later, in the Chicago Stadium. It was a bar-room brawl. This time Tony was demolished in six rounds, well and truly knocked out. Rocky said: 'If it hadn't been for the ref I'd have killed him.'

Their third fight was to take place this evening – the deciding fight. It was held in Rupert Stadium in Newark, New Jersey, because Graziano had been suspended in New York State for graft. A torrential downpour the night before had made them postpone the match. Rocky was very nervous. He attacked furiously with wide swings which Tony had no trouble blocking or dodging. A straight and well-aimed hook sent Rocky to the canvas a first time. He got up again but not for long. Tony connected with each of his blows in the third round. Rocky fell, got up, and fell again, his arms stretched out. 'Out.' Tony had won. He would take Cerdan on wherever and whenever he wanted, as soon as he had regained the European title. He gave his word.

Edith and Marcel, 10 July 1948, Brussels
It was now or never for Marcel. 'Just be yourself and you'll defeat Delannoit,' Roupp told him. 'You'll have your revenge.'

Lew Burston came over from New York with the President of the Millionaires Club, Mr Ben Bodne, who ran a New York boxing organisation which competed with the Garden, the 'champions' tournament'. Two other American journalists were also present, representing the United Press and Associated Press agencies. People in the US were becoming increasingly doubtful about the Frenchman. He wasn't ranked so highly. Even in Brussels. During his last training session, Marcel's right hand had gone again. Marcel would only be able to fight with his left hand. He would need guts to make up for his lack of punch.

Roupp had thought of everything, except Piaf. Edith had come too. Marcel had kept it from Roupp until the last moment. She managed to get a contract in Brussels itself for 12 July. Only after he had been weighed in did Marcel tell him sheepishly, 'I must go and join her, Mr Roupp.' A hook in the stomach from Cerdan would have caused Roupp less pain. He tried to reason with Marcel, urging him not to meet up with Edith. It was a reckless idea; they were surrounded by people, including journalists. The whole thing would backfire.

'Call her up and explain, Marcel.'

'I can't, Mr Roupp, I promised her.'

Roupp gave way in the end, but insisted on accompanying Marcel to Edith's hotel. Marcel was full of smiles during the journey. Roupp glared at him. He was angry with Piaf.

Loulou Barrier insisted on going to the Palais des Sports to root for Cerdan. Edith didn't watch the fight. She stayed behind in her room and prayed, waiting for Marcel's phone call. She heard the good news from him. She leapt up at the first ring. She could hear Marcel's jubilant voice at the other end. He had won in fifteen rounds.

Edith and Marcel, mid-August 1948, Anet
Edith and Ginou had collapsed in giggles. On the way to the little village of Anet in Eure-et-Loir, Edith asked Emile, the chauffeur, to slow down a bit. He was driving as though in a rally. 'Slow down, Emile, slow down. We'll get there on time.' Emile raised his foot automatically. Edith scrutinised his face. 'Tell me, Emile, what are all those scars on your face? Did you get them in the war?'

'No, madame,' he replied, without relaxing his attention, looking straight ahead and keeping his eyes on the road. 'They were accidents.'

'What do you mean, "accidents"? Car accidents? Were you injured?'

Emile kept a straight face. 'Not much. But the women who employed me . . .' Emile had a good sense of humour.

Edith and Ginou were still laughing when Emile parked the car in front of a little country inn where Marcel, Lucien Roupp, his wife and step-daughter had taken refuge for the last few days, to escape the journalists.

As soon as she got out of the car Edith rushed into Marcel's arms. He lifted her by the waist and swung her round. He was in superb shape. It was in the bag. It was signed. He would have his world championship. He had dreamed about it so often. And Edith likewise.

'It's so restful here, you have no idea. There's nothing to disturb the peace and quiet. You'll like it, I know.'

'Are they leaving you in peace?' asked Edith, referring to the journalists.

Marcel smiled, showing all his new white teeth. 'They're looking for me everywhere. They don't know where I am.'

It was a low, single-storey house built out of rough local stone, an isolated rustic house, dilapidated in parts with its rendering crumbling away. There were fields on all sides as far as you could see, and a yard with three tables and a bench in it. Roupp had booked the rooms and insisted to the inkeeper that there should be no other guests. He had reserved the biggest room for himself, his wife and his step-daughter, an attractive young girl of fourteen.

Edith and Marcel shared a very comfortable room and Ginou had one to herself.

Ginette Richer, the secretary, known as Ginou writes:

'I had never seen Edith so happy. You would have thought it was she who was getting ready for the world championship. As soon as she arrived in Anet she adopted the same regime as Marcel. Sport was a new discovery for her and she talked about it as though it had become a central element in her life. "It makes your blood circulate, it's good for you," she would say. I didn't recognise her. She even made me go on a bike ride with her. We didn't get far; we met up with a herd of cows. She decided everyone was to drink carrot juice; that was also supposed to be good for you. Marcel couldn't stand it but he didn't dare tell her. Every morning I woke him up at 7.30. I would creep into their room and shake Marcel's shoulders several times. He was a deep sleeper. Eventually an eye would open. "Come on, Marcel, get up," I would say over and over again as gently as possible. A bucket of water over his head wouldn't have made any difference. But he always woke up with a smile. "OK, Ginou? Are you feeling fit?" he would ask. Then I would hand him his carrot juice. That's when the problems began. He would grimace and say, "Why do you do this to me? It's disgusting," glancing at Edith sleeping beside him. He would get up quietly, splash himself with water and then do a few exercises to wake himself up properly. We would then meet up in the yard behind the house where the training would begin. It was an incredible scene. He would stand there alone and start to fight himself. He threw out a series of jabs, rolled his shoulders and swayed his hips. I found out this was called "shadow boxing". Afterwards, he would punch a bag of sand for fifteen rounds. I held the stop-watch. Roupp slept through it all. I would sit down under a tree and if I happened to close my eyes Marcel would immediately shout out, "Ginou, wake up. We're not here to enjoy ourselves." Then he skipped. I couldn't say how long for. I thought it would never end.

'After the training session was over we would wake up *"la p'tite"*, as he called her. When I say "we" I mean that Marcel would ask me to bring Edith round. He knew she hated waking up. I was used to it – I never raised my voice or opened the curtains. I would repeat several times, "Edith, it's time to wake up." She would get up, take off her sleeping-mask and her ear-plugs, brush her teeth, comb her hair and put on a house-coat.

107

'Edith hated to be rushed. At this point I would call Marcel. He would appear, all smiles, and I would leave them. After lunch we relaxed in the countryside and enjoyed ourselves. We played a lot of board games. Especially Monopoly. Marcel was obsessed by the rue de la Paix and the Champs Elysées. He wanted everything. He loved winning. He cheated like a child.'

Lucien Roupp kept having to make trips to Paris. The sports journalists couldn't understand Cerdan's disappearance. The newspaper offices were in turmoil. The great boxing experts who were supposed to be close to the champion were hassled by their chief editors. Roupp was in a fairly delicate position, being forced to shroud Marcel's training in mystery, against his better judgement. His attempts at reassurance didn't do anything to improve the journalists' annoyance. He was inundated with questions: 'But where is he?' 'What's he doing?' 'What's his routine?' 'What kind of shape is he in?' and 'When will we be able to see him?'

There was a hint of scandal in the air, which hadn't escaped Roupp's notice. He tried to get Marcel to change his decision to cut himself off from the world.

Edith made no attempt to hide her satisfaction when Roupp left Anet. She even provoked him by saying: 'OK, Lucien, have a good day. See you this evening. Take your time!'

Marcel didn't dare say anything. He had always been very deferential towards his manager, whom he addressed as 'Mister Roupp'. This got on Edith's nerves.

'Come on, Marcel,' she kept telling him, 'will you stop calling him "Mister Roupp" every time you open your mouth. Don't forget you're the one who gets into the ring and you're the Champion. Does he call you "Mister Cerdan"?'

Marcel nodded. But he tried to change the subject – even a dictation was preferable. Edith had taken it into her head to teach him to spell. Or, to her great delight, he would attack one of the books she had chosen. He had begun to read *In Dubious Battle* by Steinbeck. Now he was attacking André Gide, who was all the rage at the time. Piaf told him, 'He's a bright guy. He's just been awarded the Nobel Prize.' Another person would have responded, 'Who cares?' But Marcel was duly impressed. And so, reading extremely slowly, he began Gide's novel *Strait is the Gate*:

'I was born in the rue de Médicis, in a fifth-floor flat which my parents left several years later and of which I have no memory. I can however visualise the balcony or rather what you could see from the balcony: the square which was a stone's throw away and the fountain, or, to be still more precise, I can visualise the paper dragons cut out by my father which we would throw from the top of the balcony to be carried away by the wind over the fountain in the square to the Jardins du Luxembourg, where they would get caught in the top branches of the chestnut trees . . .'

Later on, when he got further into Gide's work he asked Edith innocently as he was turning a page: 'Tell me, was he a bit of a pansy, your Gide?'

Marcel waited up for Roupp one evening. Lucien was more put out than ever.

'I don't understand you, Marcel. How can you do this to them? In a month's time you're boxing in the world

109

championship, yet you're refusing any contact with the people who made you famous.'

'OK,' said Marcel. 'If you insist I'll see one, just one. Felix Lévitan. I'll call him tomorrow at the *Parisien*. Thursday would be a good day for him to come.'

Marcel had long had complete confidence in Felix Lévitan, a journalist whose writing was considered authoritative. Although he was very incisive, forceful and always to the point in his articles, Lévitan knew how to draw a line between someone's public and private life. If he was at all interested in the private life of the champions he wrote about, he kept it quiet. Lévitan had known all about Edith and Marcel from the word go. When Marcel decided to tell him about it, Felix had said, 'Marcel, it's your own life, isn't it?' And they had left it at that.

So, if he had to speak to a journalist, he would rather it were Felix. Marcel told Roupp: 'With Felix we won't run into any problems. He'll be discreet. I'll tell Edith not to worry.'

Marcel saw Roupp's face relax a bit, although he still argued: 'I agree about Lévitan, but what about his colleagues? Have you thought about the others?'

'No,' replied Marcel, 'but Edith won't agree to any other arrangement.'

Thursday 19 August: a detailed plan had been laid. Marcel told Felix over the phone that a young woman would come and meet him at the edge of the village. He described Ginou, a good-looking young brunette, with a ready smile. Felix took down all the directions: the road to Ivry la Bataille, then the main road again to the crossroads where Ginou would be waiting for him. He didn't really need these detailed instructions. As he told Marcel, 'It's a good arrangement. My brother-in-law owns a house a few kilometres from Anet.' Then he suggested to the boxer that his wife, Genevieve, come with him.

110

'Of course,' said Marcel.

Ginou enjoyed the mission. She cycled to the rendez-vous and watched out for the few cars which turned off down the country road. Then she spotted the Lévitans.

Marcel gave Felix a joyous welcome. The two men embraced familiarly. Edith came forward with open arms. Marcel had spoken highly of the Lévitans and Edith had decided that Marcel's friends would be her friends. She took to them from the beginning.

Dinner was a jubilant affair. When the time came for coffee, Marcel and Felix talked boxing in a corner of the dining-room, and Edith and Genevieve sat on the floor chatting to one another.

Edith got up. Genevieve had charmingly insisted that she put one of her records on the record-player. The music and sound of Edith's voice did not halt Felix and Marcel's 'fistic' discussion. Genevieve felt she had to intervene. She turned to the two men and interrupted them. 'How can you go on talking when Edith's singing?'

This spontaneous remark touched Edith to the quick. She rose and embraced Genevieve. It was the beginning of a great friendship.

The next day, Edith decided they would visit Lisieux, or rather St Theresa of Lisieux. 'We must go there, Marcel. I feel it in my bones.'

Marcel was easily persuaded. He knew how important St Theresa was for Edith. She had told him all about it. As a child she had suffered from a prolonged attack of conjunctivitis. She told her mother, 'Mum, my eyes are watering,' then, 'Mum, I can't see anything.' She was sent to stay with her grandmother, who ran a seedy hotel thirteen miles from Lisieux. The old lady was pious. She divided her time between prayers and the smutty jokes of her customers. One day she made Edith kneel down

111

at the feet of Saint Theresa of the Child Jesus and made her recite fervent pleas to the saint. Ten days later Edith saw the sun again.

'It was a miracle, Marcel, a real miracle.'

He was not a practising Catholic but he had got into certain habits, such as burning a candle to the Virgin before each fight.

Edith brought a little statue of her benefactor back from their visit to Lisieux. It never left her bedside.

Marcel was to leave France on 22 August for his ninth transatlantic crossing in twenty-two months. Edith, who had landed a $7,000 contract at the Versailles from 22 September, the day after the world championship, had of course planned to fly out on the same plane. Marcel spoke to Roupp about it. Roupp didn't say anything, but at the first opportunity he got in touch with his Air France friends and told them to say there was no seat for Mme Piaf on the plane.

Edith was thwarted and had to delay her flight to America until 3 September.

On the morning of Marcel's departure the house in the rue Leconte de Lisle was in a state of nervous excitement. Edith told Ginou to pack Marcel's case. She was shouting out orders: 'And whatever you do, don't forget the pullover.' It was a garish aubergine-coloured pullover; Edith had knitted every stitch with love. Solange had modelled it, walking around the flat to display it from all angles. She was kind to Edith: 'It's very beautiful, Madame . . .' It was ghastly.

When he put it on to sweat into during his training, Marcel winked at Edith: 'If I fight well, it will be thanks to your pullover. I've never had such a beautiful one.'

In the end, Edith packed the pullover herself. It was the only way to be sure. When Marcel left she began praying in her room. Ginou watched her in silence. She was touched.

All of a sudden, Edith got to her feet. 'Ginou, my dear, do you smell what I smell?'

A scent had filled the room.

'Yes, Edith, it smells like roses.'

Whereupon they heard the voice of Guy Bourguignon, Ginou's husband, as he climbed the stairs: 'What's happened? What have you broken? A bottle of perfume?'

Edith's face was ecstatic. She cried out, radiant: 'Now I know my little one will be world champion.'

Thanks to Edith, St Theresa of Lisieux had just extended her protection to Marcel.

9

The Mysterious Goings-On at Loch Sheldrake

Lew Burston's telegram left no option: 'Be here no later than 24th. Marcel must be present for the signing with Tony Zale. Will be filmed and televised.'

There was no way Marcel could get out of it. He had to accept it and abandon the idea of a few days grace with Edith. He gave in grudgingly to the demands of his American agent and, with a scowl on his face, joined Lucien Roupp at Orly. He even refused the traditional glass of champagne which the airport barman liked to offer him. All he would have was a bottle of Perrier at the counter. He seemed impatient with the time taken up with formalities.

Roupp breathed a sigh of relief when the plane took off at 11.00 p.m. and the little wooden sheds scattered about the runways disappeared from view. He was already visualising their arrival at the other end: New York, La Guardia airport, the crowds of reporters, radio, television, the signing of the contract at Gallagher's, the fashionable Broadway restaurant, all the important people who were awaiting them. America in glorious technicolor. And for Marcel, at last, the fight of a lifetime, the fight of his dreams . . .

But Roupp had let himself get carried away. The journey was a disaster. It took them five hours to reach Shannon where a faulty engine extended the stopover by another five hours. An hour later, with the tanks filled to the brim, an engine broke down completely about 250 miles from the Irish coast. There was considerable agitation when the pilot announced an abrupt about-turn. Twenty-four hours after leaving Paris, Cerdan's plane was back at its point of departure!

With an army of reporters on his hands in New York, Lew Burston was thrown by this stroke of bad luck. He was forced to improvise a makeshift press conference. 'What a shambles,' he muttered. 'These Frenchmen are just like Mexicans!' That was what he was thinking. Fortunately he wasn't short of anecdotes. To those who pressed him with questions, he was only too happy to tell the story of Marcel's first mishap in the air. It was a funny story.

It had happened before the Raadik fight. Cerdan's flight had again been delayed by a mechanical problem: an oil pump refused to work, and to make matters worse the plane had to alter course. Instead of making for Shannon it had to head south towards the Azores because of violent winds. Lew Burston was a perfectionist and always on time; it never entered his head that anything could have gone wrong. When the Constellation finally landed in New York, he had gone home long ago. There was no one to welcome Cerdan!

Lew could also have talked about Marcel's aversion to flying. This dated back to 4 November 1946 when a Portuguese paper, *Mundo Desportivo*, went so far as to predict Cerdan's death in a plane crash. It was a few weeks before the fight against Abrams. Shortly afterwards, Cerdan embarked on the *Ile de France*. Both prudent and superstitious, he had decided to travel by boat.

Following in the wake of the police car, Jo Rizzo's Cadillac went into another skid. Rizzo glanced in his rear-view mirror; Marcel was obviously enjoying himself. It was like a rodeo. Jo came to a halt in front of the security guard's booth. A local band struck up *'La Marseillaise'*. There was a banner over the entrance with the words 'Welcome Home Marcel Cerdan'. Most of the 800 guests of the Evans Hotel at Loch Sheldrake had turned out to satisfy their curiosity and welcome Marcel. The place where Marcel now found himself was a vast preserve, 100 miles from New York in the heart of the Catskills, a semi-mountainous region dotted with lakes and grand hotels. The region owed its prosperity to tourism; fashionable Manhattan doctors were prescribing outdoor rest for patients suffering from overwork. Summer brought an exodus of affluent families obeying the newspaper advertisements to 'Leave the scorching summer heat behind and take your wives and children to the mountains. Clean air. Pure water. Fresh milk.'

This choice spot had long been popular with the champions. While Marcel was moving into the hotel run by the five Evans brothers, Sugar Ray Robinson, who was training for his fight against Kid Gavilan, was resting up in a nearby hotel, the Morningside Resort.

Marcel and Lucien Roupp shared a white bungalow surrounded by a fence, below the main building. The Evans brothers had placed a brand new French flag to the right of the entrance and had even nailed up a discreet little sign over the doorway saying 'Marcel Cerdan Cottage'. There were clumps of flowers on all sides, an undulating lawn, tennis courts, a basketball field, woods, fields, and the small Evans Lake criss-crossed by boats with outboard motors.

Edith was in transit. No sooner had she arrived in New York than she had to start getting ready for her onward flight to Montreal the next day. She was off on her last joint tour with the Compagnons, a brief week of galas in

116

Quebec, 6–13 September. On her return she quickly settled Momone into the Waldorf Astoria and from her room dialled 914 for Loch Sheldrake followed by the number 434 55 00. She had learned the number off by heart. She heard Marcel's soft but distant voice at the other end: 'Is that you, Edith?'

He had just returned from a run. Lucien Roupp was about to settle the details of the afternoon's public training when, after a long embarrassed silence, Marcel turned towards him and said: 'Edith's here.'

'Oh yes, where?'

'She's renting a room in a boarding house not far from here.'

Roupp shook his head. 'And what are you planning to do now?'

'Well, go and see her, Mr Roupp . . .'

Roupp tried hard to avoid annoying Cerdan for fear of demoralising him. He forced himself to be conciliatory. He even suggested to Marcel that he should go with him, to Marcel's great surprise. Marcel was fully aware that Edith and Roupp hadn't and never would get on.

Jo Rizzo took Roupp and Marcel to see her that evening. After ten minutes on a country road going towards Monticello they drew up outside a boarding house on the edge of the village of Hurleyville.

Edith and Momone had decided this place would serve their purpose. They hadn't been able to find a bed in the big resort hotels in the area which were overcrowded at this time of year. It was an Indian summer.

Edith and Marcel hugged each other. Roupp looked away. Edith's love for Marcel was brought home to him that evening. She must have been really devoted to him to leave her fine New York suite and move into this sad, shabby little room. He could no longer be in any doubt about the nature of her feelings.

117

Happy as she was to see Marcel again, Edith was very courteous towards Lucien Roupp. She told him, confidingly: 'You know, no one knows Momone and I are here.' She laughed. 'It's a secret. I hope you're not going to give us away.' Roupp and she had never got on so well. Marcel looked happy.

Just under an hour went by in a very relaxed atmosphere. Edith bent over backwards to be polite. It wasn't her style. Roupp wondered what was going on. He quickly got the picture when Marcel whispered in Edith's ear: 'Don't worry, I'll come and see you every evening.'

Roupp's expression changed. He fiddled with his glasses. Now Edith and Marcel were going too far. 'No, Edith, it's not going to be possible. I don't think you realise how risky it would be for Marcel to leave his training camp every day at the same time. There are lots of journalists. They would soon guess what you were up to. And, Edith, aren't you yourself keen to keep it a secret? You mustn't do anything silly.' He explained to them that a single slip on their part could earn them all the fire and fury of puritan America. In this country where virtue was held in such esteem, illicit love was not taken lightly.

Roupp was a good judge of the situation but didn't manage to convince Edith, who protested vehemently. She was beginning to tire of the Americans and their morals. Roupp then realised he had to find a way out which would harm neither Edith nor Marcel. He turned to Jo Rizzo for inspiration. Rizzo was quick on the uptake: 'Of course we could move Edith into a bungalow at Loch Sheldrake.'

'What do you mean?' asked Roupp. 'Wouldn't that be very dangerous?'

'Well, I could hide myself. Don't worry, Roupp, I won't cause any trouble.' Piaf liked the solution. There was no point in discussing it any further. The next day Jo Rizzo

118

booked rooms at the hotel in the name of his sister and a friend. They would both move into the bungalow next to Marcel's. Jo then went back to Hurleyville to fetch Edith and Momone. His family had just grown.

On the way back, Jo warned Piaf to be on her guard as much as possible. 'Do be very careful, Edith. Lucien is right. They're going through a funny time here.' It was in all the papers: old Senator Johnson had come down from his mountains in Colorado to issue a warning on behalf of the virtuous majority, 'against all the apostles of degradation and the temptations of a life of debauchery'.

Rizzo turned the Cadillac onto a forest track on one of the last bends before Loch Sheldrake. He got out and asked Edith and Momone to get into the boot of the car.

'But why, Jo?' Edith asked in amazement.

'Have you forgotten about the journalists?'

'No one's ever made me do this before!' she cried while Momone sniggered.

To get in and out of the Evans Hotel you had to show your room key as a form of identification. In his Cadillac, Jo no longer had to go through this formality. He was Cerdan's chauffeur and the barrier was automatically raised for him.

Edith's life at Loch Sheldrake began. Marcel's continued. And their joint life developed with ups and downs of intensity and boredom. It was out of the question for them to be seen together in the daytime. While the sports reporters had grudgingly kept their affair quiet, in recent weeks the gossip columnists had begun to inquire into it. Some even expressed doubts about Marcel's prospects in the fight. These comments stung Edith to the quick. But for the sake of the sport, or rather, for reasons of state, Edith made a sacrifice and voluntarily adopted a sort of self-imposed clandestine existence. She shut herself inside.

119

Momone and Edith lived behind closed curtains, as though cut off from the world. They had to keep their voices down. They didn't chat; they whispered and knitted. Never before had she knitted like this. Marcel would certainly be warm that winter. She only saw Marcel in the evenings. He would bring food for a meal or rather a snack. He grabbed everything he came across. Edith had never eaten so many sandwiches. Every evening he would apologise for not being able to bring her more. Edith was only too ready to excuse him: 'Don't worry about us,' she told him, 'concentrate on yourself and your fight.' She could tell from the way he smiled that he was relieved. The only thing Edith and Momone missed a bit was wine. Sandwiches don't go down very well with water. They were on a forced diet. After eating, the three of them would play cards. Marcel always cheated a bit. He couldn't help it. They would turn a blind eye and let him win so they could enjoy his triumph. For a laugh they would sometimes play for the apéritif although there was no apéritif to be won. He would always leave around 11.00 p.m.: his bed-time. He never stayed on to sleep with Edith. Roupp had lectured him repeatedly. 'Not too much lovemaking. It wears out the legs and Zale is quick on his feet.' Besides, that wasn't why he came. All they really needed was to see each other.

All the same, Edith used to tell herself what a wonderful holiday the two of them could have had here. If she had had her way, she would have taken Marcel everywhere. There were so many attractions nearby: famous restaurants, such as the Melody Room in Monticello; or the Paddock Supper Club, well known for its Chinese cuisine; the Sugar Bowl, with its bowling lanes opposite the Kiamesha Lake; variety shows in the Rivoli Theatre in Falsburg, where the comic pair Abbott and Costello, who had recently appeared with Edith at the Versailles, were performing; and of course, the Strand Cinema in Loch Sheldrake itself. And every evening at 8.00 there were horse races. All this was to be found within a radius of seven miles. Edith ate her heart out reading about it in a guide. She confided in Momone: 'I must really have him under my skin to be living this crazy existence!'

Cerdan slipped naturally into the lifestyle of a world-title challenger. The daily routine was as follows: orange juice, running, meal, siesta, interviews, relaxation, sparring etc. But wherever he went – on the tracks for his work-out or in the ring to punch the sand-bag where a smart PR man had drawn Tony Zale's face and chest – Cerdan always wore his white Evans Hotel tee-shirt.

The Evans family had adopted Marcel from the start. Pampered, protected and cossetted, he became particularly friendly with Jacky, the youngest of the five brothers, who could speak French. After a few days at Loch Sheldrake, Marcel found himself saying: 'I have two homes: one in Casablanca and one here.' He went further and told them in his kind way: 'I'm not Marcel Cerdan. I'm Marcel Cerdan-Evans.'

This amused the Evans children no end. Little Bobby, a toughie and a fighter, reminded him of his oldest son, Marcel Junior.

They had set aside a special room for his meals. Cerdan turned it down. 'No, no, I'll eat in the dining-room with the children. It will be like being at home.' His great pastime was to swap chewing-gum for comics. Cronin, Gide and the others were temporarily shelved . . . The kids of the hotel, who wouldn't leave his side, ended up calling him Uncle Marcel.

His spontaneity and good humour delighted the journalists from the local Sunday paper, the *Sunday News Republican*, and the *Sullivan Democrat*. They called him the 'jumping frog' and marvelled at the sight of him juggling with a football.

People came to see Marcel every day. There was the dapper Georges Carpentier who had previously dropped in at the Cyo Gymnasium where Tony Zale was putting the finishing touches to his training; he had good news for Cerdan. Or Pierre de Gaulle, president of the Paris municipal council, who was visiting the Mayor of New York. He hadn't thought twice about making a two-and-a-half-hour trip to invite Cerdan to dinner. And Marcel was delighted to hear him say: 'My dear Cerdan, you are a wonderful advertisement for France. We need men like you.' He meant it.

The same applied to the comments made by Georgie Abrams and his wife. The Abrams had also come to check on Marcel's shape. They were both won over. Georgie told him: 'You're bound to win because you're faster than Zale. And I should know because my fight against you was the best of my career. Zale will try to hit you at the beginning. You'll have to guard yourself.' And Georgie's wife was in no doubt either. 'Well, I'd put my money on you.' Marcel was extremely touched.

He was even more touched when his older brother, Vincent, turned up. They hadn't seen each other for twenty-two years! Marcel was just ten and had begun to box in his father's café when Vincent left for Argentina. They had a moving reunion. Marcel had insisted on paying his plane fare from Buenos Aires.

Vincent had lost an incisor, which prevented him from pronouncing the English 'th' sound, which foreigners find difficult enough to master with a normal set of teeth. Marcel found the answer to Vincent's difficulty. He put his index finger in the hole where the tooth should have been and made Vincent repeat several of the impossible words. The gag had Jacky Evans in fits.

122

One evening, in desperation, Edith suggested to Marcel that they should go for a walk in the park. It was a risk but Marcel couldn't say no to her. Momone went with them. They didn't go far. Their fear of being caught, of being seen and recognised, made them head for home.

Edith was the first to leave for New York. Marcel followed the next day. When he left Loch Sheldrake he handed out tips left, right and centre. The Evans family had wanted to give him a present. It was going to be a boxer's robe. He refused. They insisted. He had to accept a medallion.

On 20 September, the day before the world championship, he had to undergo a public training session in Roosevelt Stadium in Jersey City. On his arrival, with his hair cut, obviously completely self-possessed and relaxed, he was pleased to meet a small crowd of fans, the French community of New York. They had brought their children and insisted that Marcel shake their hands. Touched by this unexpected enthusiasm, he spent a few minutes with them, and reassured them about the next day.

All of a sudden, someone tapped him on the shoulder. He turned round. A man was staring at him.

'You're Marcel Cerdan, aren't you?'

'Yes, why?'

'You don't recognise me?'

'No, I'm sorry.'

'You really don't remember?'

'No, I really don't.'

'I'm Eddie Ran. You defeated me a few years ago in Paris.'

The fight had taken place in the Salle Wagram on 13 January 1938. Cerdan had made Eddie Ran's acquaintance in a lively and fairly violent fashion: he had knocked him out in two rounds.

10

Roses All the Way

Edith and Marcel, 21 September 1948, New York
Marc Bonel, Piaf's accordionist, couldn't take his eyes off
Cerdan. He was amazed that just a few hours before a
fight – and what a fight for Marcel – a boxer had the
strength to talk, smile and crack jokes, in short to keep
up outward appearances as if nothing unusual was going
on. He had expected him to look wan and absent-minded,
his face a mask, and sick with nerves. But, to his astonishment, this was not the case. Marc joined Edith, Marcel,
Ginou, Lucien Roupp, Lew Burston, Jo Longman,
Marcel's brother, Vincent, and Jo Rizzo for lunch in the
apartment at 891 Park Avenue. Louise, the cook, had
prepared a light meal of little onions, steak, vegetables
and fruit. The conversation at table kept coming back to
Tony Zale. They started to discuss the weighing-in which
had taken place at midday in Jersey City.

'What a zoo!' said Marcel. 'These Americans always
have to do things their own way.'

'Eat up, darling, and don't worry about it,' answered
Edith, sounding like a woman who was beyond being
surprised by anything, particularly the Yanks, who, as
she often said, were very peculiar.

Fancy having to wait three quarters of an hour before
going onto the scales! Marcel had weighed in at 158
pounds, compared to Zale's 159 pounds.

'Did you see Zale's face?' asked Rizzo, glancing round the table deep in thought.

'What do you mean?' Marcel stopped chewing his steak. He was carefully spitting out everything except the juice.

'It may just have been an impression but I thought Zale looked pretty bad. He seemed tense, his face was yellow and he looked ill at ease. And his fans looked the same . . . a bit down. Did you notice, Marcel?'

'Well, it shows what poor actors they are!' joked Cerdan with a sparkle in his eye as he looked at Edith who was sitting on his right.

The only thing that had imprinted itself on Roupp's mind was his boxer's weight. '158 pounds!' he kept saying and, turning to Marcel, 'You haven't been as light as that for ages.'

Jo Longman agreed; his mind had been put at ease. 'Well, it's the best proof one can have that Marcel is in shape!'

'As if there could have been any doubt!' said Edith, for whom boxing no longer held any secrets. Her comment brought a smile to Marcel's face.

Lew Burston said little during the meal. He was careful not to say anything about an article he had read that morning in the *New York World Telegram* by Joe Williams. Based on bits of gossip he had dug up, and without any solid arguments, he challenged all the main world titles won by the French. He found fault with all of them: Criqui, Routis, Marcel Thil, the comical Battling Siki or Georges Carpentier who 'had paid Levinski to fight him'. From there, it was but a short step to conclude that 'Cerdan [is] the first Frenchman to fight a straightforward world championship and it would be unprecedented for France if Cerdan were to win.' It was so outrageous, so

125

prejudiced and so blinkered that it made you want to scream! Burston was almost ashamed to be American.

Williams made an effort to end on a kind note: 'When you see the Frenchman so full of smiles and so likeable you want to cry out, "Go on, Marcel!".' But the leopard can't change his spots. Williams' conclusion was: 'When I ask myself what Cerdan has that could make him win I am forced to admit that the answer is nothing!' He shared the verdict of another writer, Dan Parker of the *Daily Mirror*: 'Zale will definitely knock Cerdan out.'

Marcel had a short siesta after the meal. He was delighted to find Felix Lévitan of the *Parisien Libéré* and René Dunan of *France-Soir* in the sitting-room when he got up. The two journalists were buddies. An atmosphere of friendly familiarity now pervaded Edith's flat. They played backgammon to help pass the time. To quench his thirst, Marcel asked Louise for a glass of orange juice.

Genevieve, who had stayed behind in Paris, received the following letter from her husband Felix Lévitan:

'My Darling,
    'I am writing you this letter from Edith Piaf's apartment. It's 4.30. Marcel will be going into the ring in six hours' time. He has just won two dollars off me at backgammon. Dunan is also losing and Jo Longman, whose turn is next, is looking worried. Marcel is insatiable and is in splendid form. He wants to win the shirts off our backs and as soon as he finishes one game he starts another. We are all very excited. I know you are too in Paris. We are all thinking of you over there. I send you my love and hand over to . . .'

Edith Piaf added a few words on the back of the letter:

'How sorry I am that you can't be here to keep me

company: you are with us in spirit because your beloved husband is here, but your absence is felt and I am very sad that you can't be here. Affectionately, Edith Piaf.'

And then there was a sentence written longways down the page:

'Yes, we miss you.
Best wishes.'

It was signed Marcel.

Marcel kept up his 'splendid form' all afternoon. He won all his games of backgammon. Then, holding an ordinary Air France overnight bag, he left the apartment with Roupp and Longman. Edith went as far as the door and kissed Marcel on tip-toe. He still had the backgammon box under his arm. He had suggested to Jo Rizzo that they might play in the dressing-rooms.

Once Marcel had gone, Edith turned to Ginou, her eyes shining with pride and impatience to be at the ringside with her boxer. 'You haven't forgotten the roses, have you?'

Ginou reassured her. She had gone out herself an hour earlier to buy seven dozen dark red roses and Louise had put them in the bath to keep fresh.

'Well done,' said Edith. 'And now I'm going to have a word with St Theresa and if our friend wins, do as planned.'

Ginou understood. She didn't need to have it spelled out again. If Marcel became world champion, she would cover the floor from the lift to Edith's room with rose petals. If he didn't, she would throw them out. She was to do the same with the lace night-dress and everything

127

else that Edith had bought to honour the world champion. Either Ginou would lay it delicately on the bed or it would go straight into the rubbish bin!

Edith knelt down. Her little friend in the sky had to do something for Marcel.

Roupp was half expecting it when, on their way to the fight, Marcel asked if he could go and say a quick prayer. As they drove down Fifth Avenue before turning off for the Lincoln Tunnel, Jo Rizzo stopped the car and took Marcel into a small church. He began by lighting a candle in memory of his mother. She had died thirteen years earlier in 1935 on Marcel's nineteenth birthday. He had adored her and since then had never liked celebrating his birthday. It was the greatest sorrow of his life. Marcel had never made the sign of the cross before his mother died. But now he did it with devotion, always thinking of her. Before each fight, he had flowers put on her grave.

He then lit a second candle calling on the Virgin to watch over his fight. It was another ritual.

It was 8.30 when they reached Roosevelt Stadium. Rizzo was in the middle of Palisade Avenue and let himself be carried along by the stream of cars and taxis making for the arena. Finally, as night fell, the stadium suddenly rose up before them, shrouded in a luminous halo. It was built by the edge of the sea and had three tiers of covered terraces. There were seats in the middle of the vast arena and the ring was surrounded on all four sides by seven rows of bleachers. You couldn't help comparing it to the three miserable rows round the ring at the Palais des Sports in Paris. Here everything was on the American scale. The weather was heavy, almost humid. Ten pylons overhung the roof a good ten metres up, each bearing an impressive number of tiny spotlights directed at the ring.

They turned into the corridor leading to the dressing-rooms. Cerdan led the way, his teeth clenched. Roupp, Rizzo and Longman followed. Dr Jurmand, Edith's doctor, had also come along. He had the backgammon board under his arm.

A crowd of friends and fans had turned up to see them. They found themselves being swept along to the door of the little room. The noisy escort included George Gransford, Sugar Ray Robinson and Sammy Richman's manager, who was adviser to Holman Williams.

The elderly dressing-room attendant wasted no time in throwing out those he decided were in the way. 'You're not allowed in here. It's in the New Jersey State rules . . .'

The door closed behind Marcel. An enormous man in uniform took up position outside and prevented anyone from coming in.

Loulou Barrier chatted away in the taxi for the sake of saying something. 'I would be prepared to bet on Marcel's chances of winning in three rounds.' He knew nothing about boxing but had been won over by Marcel's friendliness. It had become a point of honour for him that Marcel should win.

Edith was in a bad state. 'Loulou, I've got the jitters for the little one,' she said in a voice petrified with fear.

Loulou turned to her. 'Keep your spirits up, Edith. Come on!'

The cars were bumper to bumper. It was hot. Through the open windows you could hear excited voices all predicting a win for Tony. It was as though these Yankees whom Edith had never hated as much as this evening were already throwing their punches at Marcel.

Marcel's room was equipped with a table and four chairs. He took some old blue trunks with white stripes out of his bag and turned to Vincent. 'Do you know what these are?' he asked his brother.

'No.'

'Mother made them for me. She said to me, "You'll win the European title in these." I've worn them ever since. And I'm going to put them on now under the white trunks the organisers have given me for the television.'

Vincent said nothing and squeezed Marcel's arm. He had been gone eight years already when their mother . . . Marcel had had the medallion of the Infant Jesus given to him by his mother sewn into the black belt of these lucky shorts which he treasured so dearly.

Marcel pulled off his clothes and put on the lavender blue robe he had already worn in all the big arenas of the world. He laced up his ring shoes himself.

The table was piled high with telegrams. Lew Burston had read them all. Appointing himself censor he automatically weeded out all those which might irritate or depress Marcel. He carefully picked out the best of them: encouragement after encouragement from faithful friends or unknown supporters, like invisible presences, egging Marcel on.

He was alone but he had never felt himself surrounded by so many people. Reverend Father Whitner in Philadelphia, whom he had met in Morocco after the landing, wrote, 'It is a great shame that my bishop has ordered me to attend a conference today. I won't be able to see you. But this morning when I said Mass, I prayed for you.' There were even letters addressed to him as 'Cerdan, world champion'.

Marcel laughed out loud. He opened an envelope which had caught his eye. He recognised the writing. He hurriedly pulled out the piece of cardboard folded in four. No one but he could have understood. Marcel, his oldest son, had sent him the message he had been expecting. It was yet another superstition going back to his adolescence. At sixteen he had seen *The Champ*, an unadulterated melodrama starring Wallace Beery and Jacky Cooper. A champion, reeling from blows, and about to go under, finally triumphed when his kid came into his corner and spat into his glove. Cerdan had been deeply moved by the scene.

Some time later Marcel also found himself in a tough fight against an opponent who was heavier and more ruthless than he was. Despite the exhortation of his friends, Marcel was boxing half-heartedly. He was in his opponent's hands and defeat seemed inevitable. The film came back to him like a flash during one of the rest periods. He turned to his best friend, Louis Lopez, and said, without thinking, 'Spit into my glove!' A bit taken aback, his friend did as he was told. And a miracle took place. Marcel pulled off one of the finest knock-outs of his career. It established a tradition which then became almost a superstition. For many years Louis Lopez continued his good offices. Then Marcel Junior took over. Tonight again it would enable him to ward off the evil eye.

There was also a telegram which read 'Hit him hard, daddy', signed: 'Marcel, René, Paul'.

He stuffed the telegram into the pocket of his robe. There was a knock at the door. It was Sam Pian, Zale's manager, who had come to check on the bandages on Marcel's hands. Billy West, attached to the French side, went off to do the same to Zale.

Night fell over the stadium, thick and black, and it grew a little cooler. The stewards were affable and understanding. In the middle of the ground, under fifty white lights, the ring looked like an operating table. The preliminary fights were under way when Edith took her place in the second row of ringside seats. She was lost in the anonymity of the crowd. There were few if any camera flashes. The photographers had gathered round the blonde Sonja Henie, the former Olympic figure-skating champion who had become a Hollywood star. Her shoulders were bare and her figure slender. Sonja was posing. Edith didn't notice her. She was sitting next to Ginou. The others, Momone, Loulou Barrier and Marc Bonel, were nearby. At the last moment, however, Bonel had to give up his ringside seat to Dr Jurmand. Bonel was relegated to the back of the terraces. He grumbled a bit. It was a dreadful sacrifice for him; he was still dazzled at finding himself in Cerdan's entourage. But the accordionist was lower in the hierarchy than Edith Piaf's doctor so he had to move away. He found himself in the cheap seats packed tight with Zale's staunchest fans. He kept quiet. He had never altered his watch. He was still living on French time. It was the only way he could stop himself from feeling like a fish out of water.

Not far from Piaf were Fernandel, who had arrived that day and was staying over in New York before flying on to Quebec; the Parisian manager Gaston Charles Raymond and his heavyweight boxer Weidin, who had both come from Baltimore; and the racing cyclists Grauss and André Pousse. Marcel's friends, the Compagnons de la Chanson, were missing. They were appearing that evening at the Directoire, one of the top Broadway night-spots. They hadn't been able to take a break. They apologised to Marcel, deeply disappointed.

'Cerdan, it's your turn.' One of the organisers of the Tournament of Champions put his head round the door. Marcel broke off his warming-up exercises. He was white as a sheet. He adjusted his gown and draped a towel over his head. Roupp grabbed him by the shoulder.

'Start off the way I told you. Cover yourself and use your right to block him when you can.'

A light wind swept over the ring from the nearby sea. The Master of Ceremonies, dressed in a dinner jacket, was taking his time introducing all the champions present to the public. There was Billy Conn, Gene Tunney, Georgie Abrams, Lee Savold, Charles Fusari, Tippy Larkin, Virmellie Bettina, Bob Ollin and Billy Roose, the former holder of the middleweight title. When Gus Lesnevitch's name was announced the twenty thousand spectators yelled and stamped their feet. Gus should have been on the bill to fight against Joe Walcott. At the last minute the organisers did their sums: if half of the income of $240,000 went to Zale and $40,000 to Cerdan, they wouldn't have enough to pay the fees of the two semi-stars. Gus had to drop out.

Edith pummelled Ginou's arm. She was getting impatient. She was tiring of this procession of dolled-up boxers whose names meant nothing to her and who made her laugh. 'Who are all these guys?' she whispered.

All of a sudden there were yells and screams. The spectators rose to their feet. Tony Zale appeared in a white gown with a towel draping his head. Marcel rose up on the other side, with Roupp and Burston. Roupp was wearing a white, loosely woven shirt, like a tennis player's, with 'Marcel Cerdan' on it in red letters. The boxers put on their gloves. Edith tried to focus her attention on Marcel. They played 'La Marseillaise'. She rose. Everyone stood to attention. Then Alan Bell sang the American national anthem in his mellow voice, to the accompaniment of an accordionist.

She could see him . . . Edith shivered with cold and anxiety. How anxious he seems, she said to herself. She was wrong.

Marcel listened but didn't understand the instructions of the American referee. His name was Paul Cavalier, a curiously French-sounding name. He ran through the rules in force in the State of New Jersey. Lew Burston translated: the manager is not entitled to throw in the sponge; if a boxer falls to the ground he must be counted eight before starting the fight again. Cerdan wasn't bothered. He couldn't envisage either of these things happening.

In the press section people were already fighting with the Western Union telegraphists to send out the first cables. Reporters sent out specially by the French media included René Dunan, Gaston Bénac, Felix Lévitan, Georges Février, Georges Peeters, Pierre Crenesse, a radio reporter and the New York correspondents of the main newspapers – George-Henri Martin, André Rabache and Jean Kroutchtein. Their American colleagues chewed their cigars exuberantly. They were less excited, but shouted out to each other noisily, and all agreed Zale would win – all, that is, but two of them: Jimmy Cannon of the *New York Post* and Leslie Bromberg of the *New York World Telegram*. They had decided to play the odds. The bookmakers had put Zale at 8.5–1 compared with 5–1 for Cerdan.

The bell rang out. It was 10.15. Marcel crossed himself furtively. Edith's face was drawn and white. Without thinking, she called on Saint Theresa again. Zale opened by hitting out. Marcel responded with hooks, and circled Zale. Accurate, quick and keeping his guard up he fought it his way, sticking to the approach he had chosen. From behind his closed guard he threw a left to the stomach and a right to the face. Edith breathed again.

Bell. Rest. Edith saw Marcel suck in his stomach. Marcel

was taking deep breaths; his shoulders were rising and falling rhythmically. Edith thought he looked good.

The fight started again. Zale tried to take the initiative but failed. Marcel's arms formed a shield which caught Tony's fists. When they emerged from a clinch Marcel delivered a right to the American's temple. Zale grimaced. Edith was in seventh heaven. Zale retreated.

The bell went. They spent most of the next round quietly observing each other. Almost too late, at the end of the round, Zale deflected a right from Cerdan. Marcel far outclassed his opponent in technique and speed. Zale realised what he must do: knock Marcel down as quickly as possible. Cerdan complained about a punch below the belt.

Bell. A left–right combination from Marcel. Then Zale delivered a magnificent hook to Cerdan's jaw. There was a sharp crack. Edith felt as though the blow had landed on her own face. She threw herself back. Cerdan's knees buckled. Edith's blood froze. Marcel wavered. He was stunned. He couldn't see straight. Edith dug her nails into her skin. All around her the Americans were going wild: 'Come on Tony! C'mon! Kill the frog!' Marcel put his arms round Zale's neck and pressed his head into the champion's shoulder. Edith clung to Ginou. 'Tell me it's not true!' She tensed her shoulders and closed her eyes. She opened them again, remembering something Marcel had told her. Before the fight, to attract publicity, someone had wanted Marcel to say that he would defeat Zale in five rounds. Marcel refused. It wasn't his style.

Marcel gradually recovered. The storm passed. Edith separated herself from Ginou. The bell went.

The smelling salts bucked Marcel up. The danger was over. He resumed his efforts, keeping his distance. Edith felt calmer and settled back into her chair, reassured. Marcel was back on form. Zale couldn't get over it. He

135

showed signs of fatigue. Marcel stepped up his efforts. Edith stamped her feet and hit the hat of the spectator sitting in front of her.

The bell went. The man turned round. He assumed Edith was crazy and shrugged his shoulders. Edith paid no attention. 'Go on, Marcel!' She was white as a sheet. He was quite pale. He altered his pace, put more weight into his blows and advanced on Zale. 'Mar-cel! Mar-cel!' He was delivering hooks with both arms. The man's hat got hit again! He realised there was nothing he could do. The fight went on. All Cerdan's blows struck home. It was a demolition job. Left, left, left. And left again. 'Your right, Marcel!' But Marcel couldn't hit with his right any more. He had hurt it. Edith bit her fist.

The bell went. There were strident whistles from the spectators. Insatiable, they wanted more of the same, immediately. Her ears were ringing. Marcel was giving a star performance. Zale was crouching against the ropes. Cerdan wanted to finish him off. Zale hung on, bending under the avalanche of blows and returned to his corner in a daze.

The bell went again for the eleventh round. Cerdan delivered a left hook. Zale had blood in his mouth. Marcel stepped up the pressure. He quickened the pace. Zale's legs gave way. The man's hat was knocked right off his head this time. Marcel attacked again with both fists and struck Zale on the chin with a left. Zale was still standing. Marcel danced from foot to foot. Edith fidgeted. There was a splendid left hook. Zale staggered, but hung on. Two lefts to the face. Wild-eyed, Zale fell to his knees. The referee intervened to help bring Zale back into his corner. Cerdan said to himself, 'That's it.'

'You've won, Marcel!' cried out Edith.

The bell went. Zale didn't get off his stool. Edith leapt up. The referee raised Marcel's arms, Edith threw herself into the arms of Ginou, Momone and Barrier. The man in front laughed and handed her his battered hat. 'Keep this as a souvenir.'

The Master of Ceremonies grabbed the microphone and shouted through the uproar: 'The Frenchman is champion of the world.'

'Marcel, you're world champion. Do you realise?' Edith was weeping softly.

Ginou didn't stay to see the ring invaded, or the police fighting with spectators or Marcel receiving the sincere congratulations of the former world champion – Tony was a true sportsman. She rushed off to find a yellow cab and get back to the flat. She followed Edith's instructions, spreading the roses from the lift to the bedroom. In he middle of the carpet of flowers she laid down the cardboard signs lovingly painted by Marc Bonel with small, painstaking brush strokes: 'Congratulations, Marcel Cerdan', 'Long live our world champion', 'Hurray for Marcel'.

Edith and Marcel finished the evening in a relaxed fashion at the Directoire where a large oval table had been reserved for them, their friends and the Compagnons. They returned to the apartment on Park Avenue at two in the morning.

Marcel was overwhelmed at the sight of the red-carpet treatment which awaited him. He was dazed. He gripped Edith's hand. 'But it's all too much.'

Ginou watched them both, moved. She wanted to cry. Edith saw and said, 'Come on, Ginou. Give Marcel a kiss. He deserves it.' Ginou embraced both of them and then disappeared.

Edith and Marcel settled onto the big divan in the sitting-room. Vincent and Felix Lévitan were still there. Louise brought some whisky and poured it out for them.

Marcel's face looked bruised but he assured his brother that Zale hadn't hurt him once.

'But he hits hard, you know.'

'As we saw in the fourth round.'

'It started with a bang. I saw a sort of flash.'

Edith was listening to them. She was spellbound.

He went on: 'But after that, every time we got into a clinch, I felt he was in difficulty. He was puffing. He couldn't keep it up. And I kept saying to myself, "I'm going to get you, I'm going to get you!" '

At three o'clock Marcel was still going over the match. Then he got up and announced, 'I'm going to bed.' Felix and Vincent saw him lie down on the sofa in the bedroom. The two brothers embraced again and Marcel said: 'To think I'm world champion.'

They turned out the light. Edith had an image in front of her eyes, the last image of the fight:

'Marcel, I saw you fall to your knees.'

'Of course, Edith, it was to thank the Good Lord.'

11

The Wheel of Fortune

He woke up shortly after midday. A few rays of sunlight were filtering in through the shutters. His left eye was swollen and black and his forehead covered with bruises. Edith couldn't get over it; he reassured her. But when he tried to get up he let out a small cry. His groin hurt. He found standing difficult. There was a touch of concern in Edith's glance which he dismissed with a peal of laughter: 'For a world champion I can't be a very beautiful sight!'

'You can say that again!' She laughed and kissed him.

Marcel then noticed that his hand didn't hurt so much any more. The pain which had made him think he had fractured it had practically disappeared: 'See, it's already better.'

They weren't alone for long. Friends soon came to join them for lunch. Jo Rizzo arrived with a bundle of newspapers under his arm. There were detailed accounts of Cerdan's triumph. He had made all the headlines. Cerdan had taken America by storm. Rizzo drew the *New York Daily News* out of the pile. Half the front page was taken up with a photo of Zale against the ropes, doubled up with his arms hanging at his side. The paper was full of similar pictures.

It was an exuberant lunch. Edith and Marcel then spent a quiet afternoon in Piaf's flat.

Edith had her première that evening at the Versailles.

139

She was returning to Broadway, some three hundred days after her chilly reception at the Playhouse. This time she wanted to be properly acknowledged. She threw herself, body and soul, into the conquest of America. The Versailles had already provided her with an opportunity to re-establish herself from nothing. She had pulled it off. Now she would be trying to win recognition for a style, an art.

Robert Chauvigny turned up for the last rehearsal. Edith sang for her own pleasure with her elbows on the piano and her head in her hands. Her songs would arrange themselves automatically in the evening.

Cerdan watched and listened in fascination. Then, without any prompting from him, she started to talk about fear and stage fright: 'You see, when I have something to do I go ahead and do it. Only afterwards do I say: "Oh dear! What if . . ." '

'What about the audience?' asked Marcel.

'I think about them. Who wouldn't? Especially here. But I'm not frightened. I know how to face up to my responsibilities. Besides, they'll clap when I appear on stage.'

Marcel had never felt himself so close to Edith. Deep down they were in the same profession. Yesterday was his day, today was hers. She nibbled at something and said, 'Let's go!' After giving him the once-over she added, 'You know, you look good like that.'

He acquiesced with an embarrassed smile. It had been a struggle getting him to buy this black dinner jacket made by Morenzi. It was his first. And Marcel would never make light of it.

They arrived together at the Versailles on the corner of 50th Street over an hour before the show was due to begin. Edith took Marcel to her dresssing-room. It was a small room on the first floor of the night-club. People streamed in. Provys, the director, couldn't have been more attentive towards Edith. He told her how fantastic it was: people had been reserving tables for the last month and he had changed his traditional arrangements for her and erected a large platform to make it easier to see her.

Momone and Ginou took turns unpacking her bits and pieces. In ten minutes the dressing-room was full of the people, things and smells associated exclusively with Piaf. Marcel tried to take up as little space as possible, so as not to be in the way. He sat himself down in a corner and looked around him in silence. She looked so extraordinarily small and slender that she reminded him of a delicate child. She made herself up. She gave him the odd conspiratorial wink in the mirror. He looked into her eyes. It was hard to say what colour they were. They seemed to change. One moment they would be blue, the next green, the next grey. It was amazing. Her eyes were eloquent but the message changed constantly, depending on what was going through her head at any moment.

The dressing-room was humming with activity. Everyone felt a mixture of confidence and nerves. Provys wished it were all over. Clifford Fischer had been to sample the atmosphere front of house. He decided the audience was ready. Barrier made conversation, as he had the day before on the way to Roosevelt Stadium. He, of course, was prepared to lay money on Edith . . .

Edith listened to them all. Marcel continued to observe the scene. The minutes ticked by. Finally, Edith was asked to go onto the stage. Discreet as ever, Marcel made himself scarce. When he reached the table which Provys had reserved for him and his guests – Charles Trénet, Georges Carpentier, Jo Longman and Sonja Henie – the champ was cheered but then they had to be quiet.

Edith appeared. She had one of the strongest voices ever heard, in one of the smallest bodies ever seen. As before, she sang to the Americans about cheap hotel rooms, lost love, eternal hopes. She opened her arms like two unfurled wings to give herself to them, and this time the American audience gave her their hearts in return.

'The striking thing', wrote the American journalist Nerin E. Gun, 'is the silence which follows the announcement of Madame Edith Piaf's name.'

The ovation began as soon as the audience caught sight of her minute figure, so breathless and frail. She acknowledged it in her characteristic manner, standing stock still and giving little nods. They were under her spell. She had the audience with her.

Edith stood there in her black dress, alone in front of the curtain and quite still in the spotlight, and began by singing 'C'était une histoire d'amour' before murmuring a short poem in American English. She then sang 'Monsieur le Noble', telling the story in English first. Edith's English was now comprehensible and quaint. There were no more of the irritating interventions made the previous year by the Master of Ceremonies. There was no longer any call for them. Americans rarely deign to be quiet during a show, let alone stop ordering drinks, but the bar service came to a halt for Piaf and people sat there enthralled, and listened, their hearts softened by what they heard. Her performance was punctuated by shouts of admiration. They shouted 'Encore!' after each song. There was another American tune and then 'Le fanion de la Légion'. The effect was instantaneous: the audience was electrified.

Then Edith gave equally magnificent performances of 'La vie en rose' and 'L'accordéoniste'. Each song was greeted with rounds of applause. All over the room people began to request their favourite songs. There were cries of 'Pigalle' from one corner. Others wanted 'De l'autre côté de la rue'. It was reminiscent of the great evenings at the

142

Club des Cinq, the Ambassadeurs or the Théâtre de L'Etoile. The applause went on and on. Some young women got so carried away in their enthusiasm that they climbed onto the tables. They wouldn't let Edith go. She then sang 'Monsieur Saint-Pierre' to a stunned audience and 'A toi, ô mon amour'. People went on clapping long after the show ended in the hope of making Edith come back and sing one last song.

The reviews were ecstatic. It was American-style enthusiasm: 'She represents the down-trodden of the world . . .' 'She brings something to our world which makes you believe in the UN.' 'Until now, the French stars we have seen had the sophisticated "Gay Paree" image, all playing on their sex appeal. Thank God for Piaf . . . She is a great artiste with a voice which really gets to you . . . a wan little girl who has obviously known hunger and suffering. She looks a little frightened . . . One could say that she typifies the new European generation, which is so worthy of our help . . .'

There was something mysterious about her magnetic presence. 'It is hard to imagine anyone as lacking in physical attraction as Mlle Piaf,' noted Bert McCord in the *New York Herald Tribune*. 'She is not at all pretty; she has none of the superficial qualities which matter so much in the world of show business, but she has such spiritual power that everything she does makes her beautiful.'

Marcel, world champion and Edith, champion of 50th Street, were deeply in love.

Marcel didn't realise what an impact his victory over Tony Zale had had in France, despite the fact that Monsieur Chancel, the French consul in New York, invited him out and told him, and Pierre de Gaulle gave a cocktail party in his honour, where the French colony thronged round him. He didn't exactly enjoy all these social obligations. New York treated him like a big celebrity, with warm, demonstrative familiarity. A few days earlier the American journalists were writing him off. Now they fought over him. He was hailed in all the newspaper offices as a long-time friend: 'Hello, champ!' and the champ smiled back at those who had been prepared to put all their money on Tony the day before.

On the morning of 23 September he found himself on 42nd Street, the press quarter, in the middle of an idle, noisy, colourfully dressed crowd. The air was filled with strong smells and a cacophony of sounds, including an attempt at the blues. It was here that Marcel realised how his reputation had soared. Many of the people he came across recognised him and said hello or waved at him. Wherever he went people gave him the thumbs up. He ended up hailing a taxi. The driver identified him at first glance and immediately launched into a feverish commentary which didn't stop until they reached 891 Park Avenue, at which point Zale had dropped to the floor, wiped out. Marcel had relived his fight and won it a second time over. The driver was still shaking his head saying 'Tony's finished' when Marcel handed him his tip.

That evening he found himself at the ringside again, in the company of Jo Rizzo, Jo Longman, Lucien Roupp and his brother, Vincent. Cerdan was delighted to do his bit by going to the Yankee Stadium to watch the Robinson-Galivan fight. He wasn't very impressed by Sugar Ray's victory.

But Marcel only really relaxed when, leaving the world of boxers and boxing behind, Jo Rizzo would drive Edith and him around in his Cadillac. You could count on Jo. There was no one like him for finding quiet spots or restaurants in the vicinity of New York where you didn't have to hide yourself from people's stares. But one day, for a change, Jo dropped them in the middle of the crowds on Coney Island. They had driven in the Cadillac to Ocean Parkway, south-west of Brooklyn, the most popular bathing resort on the East Coast, a place of cheap amusements. Marcel was astounded by the gigantic parachute tower in the funfair. People were queuing at the ticket office, hankering for the overpowering, dizzying feeling of falling 200 feet in a parachute nacelle. Edith was thrilled by the scenic railway, the big dipper and the big wheel. They were like two children. They *were* two children. They held hands. If it wasn't '*la vie en rose*', it was something very close to it. Some children approached Marcel saying 'Hello, champ'. Marcel suggested paying for them to go on the merry-go-round. Edith couldn't find the words to describe how she felt about his idea . . . She was intimidated by so much kindness, perhaps because she had a lot to learn in this field.

Unfortunately, new complications awaited them when they got back. In his down-to-earth way, Lucien Roupp reminded Marcel of his responsibilities: 'Have you given any thought to all those people back home in France who are waiting to see you?'

Roupp thought Marcel was being rather offhand. He probably lived in fear of some indiscretion on Marcel's part that would knock his good image for six. But his reaction was almost certainly motivated by his obsessive fear that Marcel would leave him. Edith was taking up more and more room in his life. Every afternoon, Roupp would find them together in the Park Avenue apartment, usually in the company of Jo Rizzo and Jo Longman. The scene was always the same: Marcel would be slumped on the floor, playing backgammon. And Edith would come and go, serene and light-hearted.

The relationship between Marcel and Roupp had taken a turn for the worse. Marcel was keeping his distance. Roupp's orders were starting to get him down. He ended up by asking him: 'Tell me, who's world champion, you or me?'

Roupp kept on stressing the need to go back to Paris. It irritated Marcel and infuriated Edith. A fight was now inevitable.

On Tuesday 28th, when Vincent Cerdan left for Buenos Aires, Marcel and Tony Zale were invited by Nat Fleischer to a lunch in their honour. Fleischer did things in style. He gave both boxers world-championship belts. Marcel was momentarily puzzled. But there was a simple explanation: Zale's belt was a belated recognition of his win against Rocky Graziano.

Tony's face was still swollen that afternoon. He didn't say much, unlike Sugar Ray Robinson who insisted on being seated next to Cerdan at table. Thanks to Jo Rizzo, they had a long conversation. The other guests included Jack Dempsey, Georges Carpentier, Abe Green, Colonel Eagan and Ike Williams, the world lightweight champion. Jo Longman came along as Marcel's chaperon. Roupp had cried off, sick. . . .

Two days later he had recovered. They were finally leaving for France. Edith, Rizzo and the Compagnons de la Chanson had insisted on accompanying Marcel to La Guardia airport. The departure was a weight off Roupp's mind, but Marcel was less happy about it.

Edith leaned forward for a kiss. His eyes made her melt. He whispered: 'I'll be back soon.'

In the plane Felix Lévitan came and sat down next to Marcel, as though he had sensed that the champion was feeling sad. Felix tried to arouse his interest in the welcome that awaited him at Orly. He was in a position to know about it. The sports editor of the *Parisien Libéré* had issued the instructions himself from New York.

Marcel was to be given a welcome surpassing his wildest dreams.

'What have you been cooking up?' asked Marcel.

'You'll see, it's a surprise. I think we've done you proud.'

Marcel was in no doubt of this. He knew Felix held him in great esteem.

'You'll never guess what lengths I've been to,' said Lévitan.

There was a silence.

Felix went on: 'I've even got them to fly our Constellation as low as possible over Paris so that people will be able to see you arrive.'

'You're crazy!' smiled Cerdan. He turned away, his mind elsewhere. 'You know, I already miss her. It's amazing. She weighs one third of what I do. I could knock her flat with one puff. Fancy such a tiny woman having such a big voice. I can't get over it.'

Felix listened to him talking about Piaf for a few minutes. Marcel was confiding things he had kept bottled up for a long time. Roupp would never understand. 'I've had enough. I'm not a machine . . . I'm a man. No one ever listens to me. I'm ordered to hit and get hit. That's all I'm good for. It's been going on for fifteen years. I've had enough.'

Felix realised that Marcel was a changed person, but he was still taken aback. Marcel wanted to unburden himself. He had often spoken to Edith about it. She had helped him see things more clearly.

'I don't care what fantastic propositions people come up with, I'll still refuse. I know full well what I want . . .'

Felix listened attentively.

'As you know,' Cerdan went on, 'I don't want to wind up crazy. It hurts getting hit. My head is still in one piece and I want to keep it that way. I swear to you I shall soon

147

drop everything and devote myself to my children. I want them to have the good start in life I never had.'

Marcel was constantly lamenting his lack of education. Felix knew the speech by heart. Marcel suffered greatly from this 'complex'. As he grew older he had come to realise how frustrating it was to hear people talk nonsense, know it was nonsense and have to keep quiet because one couldn't put one's views into words. 'I can't tell you how often that has upset me. It's sad not to be able to express what you feel inside. That's why, Felix, I don't want my sons to be in the same position. I want them to have a good education. My dream is to see all three of them, Marcel, René and Paul, pass the baccalauréat. They are being brought up to speak two languages: French and Spanish. I want them to learn English as well, so they can go anywhere in the world and make themselves understood. Later on I would like them to have their own books. I want them to have everything, do you understand?'

At 11.10 exactly the Constellation FBA-ZL touched down at Orly. It was an hour late and the humming of its four powerful engines merged with the roar of welcome from the crowds, who were held back behind white barriers.

People had been gathering quietly since 8.00 in the morning. The faithful fans had arrived in cars and on bikes. Nearby factories had stopped work especially so that the workers could be there. At first there had been hundreds of people, now there were thousands. Their long wait was rewarded when the first long-haul planes arrived and the passengers disembarked, shivering in the morning air, which was still cold despite a few rays of sunshine.

But when the big four-engined plane appeared on the far horizon no one needed to hear it announced over the loud-speakers: Cerdan was on board. It landed so near the crowds that they felt the gust of air from the propellers on their faces. A figure appeared at the top of the mobile gangway and a cry went up from the crowd. But it wasn't him. It was another passenger, followed by some more, who hurried away in embarrassment. Finally, they caught a glimpse of the world champion, looking a bit pale, his mouth tense with emotion. The crowd stamped their feet and pressed against the barriers. Claude Bellanger went forward to congratulate Cerdan on behalf of the Parisian press association. A car was waiting for Cerdan at the foot of the gangway.

Maurice Fonsèque, who was then an editor at the *Parisien Libéré*, writes:

'It wasn't any old car. It was the car Hitler had driven in when he visited Paris. We had found it at the time of the Liberation in the Petit Parisien garage. It was a black convertible. Marcel sat in the back with Lucien Roupp and Monsieur Grémaux, President of the Fédération Française de Boxe (French Boxing Federation). The car was driven by Jean Forques, our chief editor. I had gone to a lot of trouble to set up this prestigious operation. Felix Lévitan had sent the word over from New York. "Do what you like," he told me, "but put on a good show for him." I must admit I spent a few hair-raising days. I had to go to the Préfet de Police (Chief Commissioner of the Paris Police), then the Ministère de l'Intérieur (Ministry of the Interior). The bureaucracy took a long time. Eventually, I got permission to organise a motorcade through Paris. The route we followed that day had been meticulously laid down by the police: Orly, Place d'Italie, avenue des Gobelins, rue Gay-Lussac, Jardins du Luxembourg, boulevard Saint Michel, then the left bank to Place de la Concorde, Place de la Madeleine, Place de l'Opéra and along the big boulevards to the Place de la République, and the Place de la Bastille. We then drove along the rue de Rivoli to the Hôtel de Ville (City Hall) where the motorcade ended. A motorbike preceded the procession by a quarter of an hour, bearing a banner reading "Cerdan's here". There were three police motorcyles in front of Marcel's car, two on each side, and two more to bring up the rear. We were completely hemmed in by the crowds at the Place de l'Opéra. People tried to climb on to the car. Marcel kept shaking hands and thanking people. He lost a gold cuff link in the crush. Roupp was very discreet. He didn't move. After the Place de l'Opéra we turned into the rue du Quatre Septembre and drove past the newspaper offices. We had to stop every ten metres. At the Hôtel de Ville, Marcel was met by the President of the Conseil Municipal (Town Council). After this the cavalcade broke up.'

The next morning there was the inevitable reception for Marcel at the Fédération Française de Boxe. Taking the floor, Lucien Roupp turned to Marcel and, to everyone's amazement, said: 'Will you state publicly that there is no disagreement between us?' This short sentence sent ripples of concern through the room.

There were puzzled glances. Marcel blushed and people noticed he was clenching his fists as he replied, 'No, of course not.' People nudged each other. Roupp had thought he might be able to silence a few rumours this way but had managed to trigger everything off instead . . .

After Paris it was Casablanca. It was the same all over again: the airport, the motorcade, the speeches, the lunches, the cocktail parties . . . A repeat performance of Paris but on a smaller scale and more intimate and moving. General Juin, the French *'résident général'* in Morocco, appointed Marcel to the Order of Ouissam Alaouite. It was a week of celebrating and relaxing on his farm at Sidi Marouf. But it was only a short break. Marcel was summoned back to Paris for more grandiose ceremonies.

On 12 October he went to the Elysée where President Vincent Auriol presented him with a medal showing a boxer knocking out his opponent. The President's grandchildren arrived home from school unexpectedly, adding to the family atmosphere of the reception. They joined the audience, immediately recognised Cerdan and brought the house down by calmly proceeding to challenge him with clenched fists.

That evening, Marcel walked up the Champs Elysées with Marcel Hansenne, the world kilometre recordholder, and Buhan, twice Olympic fencing champion, followed by detachments from all the sports federations. All three of them rekindled the flame of the Unknown Soldier and then went off to the 'Vel d'Hiv' to participate in the 'Champions' Night'. People had come to pay their respects to no less than fifty champions.

The next evening saw a change of décor, atmosphere and dress. Stars from all over the world came to the Opéra for the *Bal des Petits Lits Blancs*. When he had spoken to Edith in New York she had insisted that he should participate in the show. She had asked her friend Jean Cocteau to arrange it. Everything would be fine. He spluttered a few words – his complex again – to the effect that Roupp didn't want him to go, and he wasn't the only one with reservations. As usual, she said Roupp could get lost and dismissed his arguments. 'Everything will be fine,' she repeated.

'And you, how are you?' he asked her.

She sounded excited. 'You have no idea. It's madness. I don't know what I've done to them. If I were to listen to them, these Americans would end up driving me crazy.' Since Marcel's departure, Edith had been asked to do a tour of various American states – Connecticut, Maine and others whose names she had forgotten.

'And what are you planning to do?' Marcel asked her.

This time, Edith could hardly stop herself from singing: 'See you again. Soon.'

The show at the Opéra that evening was a dazzling affair. For the second time in his life, Marcel wore a dinner jacket. Seated next to Louis Jouvet, he admired the array of talent. The performers consisted of all the most famous artists – all the big names in the cinema and theatre were there. Their acts were introduced by Nita Rayas, François Périer and Jean Desailly. Madeleine Renaud, Jean-Louis Barrault, Arthur Rubinstein, Espina Cortez, Germaine Sablon, Maurice Chevalier and Jean Cocteau appeared on stage one after another.

When it was Chevalier's turn, Marcel joined in. He sang along with Maurice: '*Ça va, ça va, ça va.*' And everything went swimmingly as Edith had predicted. Everything continued to go extremely well indeed when Cocteau introduced 'the poet of boxing' to all the ladies and gentlemen present.

Marcel read as much Cocteau as he could; it made him feel close to Edith, so far away in New York. Edith in turn couldn't stop thinking about him and trying to imagine him in a world which wasn't his natural milieu but in which he so wanted to make his mark.

'Look at this little woman. Her hands look like lizards darting over the ruins. Her forehead is Napoleonic; her eyes are like those of a blind woman who has

152

recovered her sight. What will it be like when she sings? How will she express herself? How will this tiny person project the powerful laments of the night? And then she sings. Like the April nightingale she ventures the first notes of her song of love. Have you ever heard the efforts of the nightingale? It strains, it sets your teeth on edge, it makes a scraping noise, it chokes. It starts and stops. And then suddenly it sings. And you are captivated.'

Marcel read these lines over and over again. He wanted to submerge himself in this description of the woman 'who is the symbol of the romantics who still know how to love, to suffer and to die.'

This was how Jean Cocteau described Piaf in his book *Le foyer des artistes*. Marcel read the words over and over again as though to let their music soak into him.

In a letter to Genevieve Lévitan, New York, 25 October 1948, Edith wrote:

'My Dear Friend:
'If Marcel had been a complete nonentity I wouldn't have loved him. He has touched my heart with his extraordinary qualities. Education and intelligence are two completely separate things. Think how many people have learned to read but don't know how to read. Give Marcel a good book and you'll see, he'll keep going when you have stopped. Which goes to prove that Marcel has risen to great heights and those who can't follow have only themselves to blame.

'He was only too well aware of his deficiencies and was the most miserable person on earth if he found himself unable to respond when people spoke to him. It was because he was aware of everything

I could do for him in this respect that he loved me so much . . .

'Marcel has always suffered from an inferiority complex which is gradually disappearing. And he wouldn't have been so magnificent if he hadn't known beforehand why that was essential. So he enjoyed his triumph to the full, knowing full well that one day this enthusiasm would dry up. It would have been dangerous if he hadn't known that one day it would all come to an end. There are many who don't know when to call it a day. Marcel will be philosophical enough and he will enjoy watching his sons grow up to become men worthy of their father. I will make sure of it! I will look after his future and I have the feeling that he will be able to find joy elsewhere than in fame.

'It is the first time in his life that Marcel has been happy. And believe me, there's no one in this world who cares more about his happiness than me.

'And I hope those who didn't bother to come and see him off but were in the first row when he made it keep out of his way, so that he doesn't suffer because of them later on.

'But this is a difficult subject to deal with in a letter. It will be easier to talk about it.

'Deep down, no one knows Marcel, and people often confuse simplicity with stupidity.

Love and kisses
Edith'

154

12

The Man with Hands of Clay

Marcel had put on weight as a result of all the celebrations and receptions and the easy life. But he didn't let the three extra kilos worry him. He was in no hurry to defend his title. He wasn't in very good shape but he was happy. He left Casablanca on the pretext of a planned exhibition bout in the US. He even forced Roupp's hand to get him to speed things up. Roupp sent a cable to Lew Burston: 'Urgent you find exhibition bouts for Marcel. Is keen to earn money and make most of title as world champion.'

They soon had a reply from Burston. He told Roupp that Marcel should pack his bags. Lew had already found two tailor-made opponents for the champ: Dave Andrews for a fight in Lewinston and Cosby Linson for a fight in New Orleans. Cerdan was to make $110,000 out of the tour.

But Marcel was really in a hurry to get back to Edith.

He embarked alone for New York on Thursday 18 November. Roupp didn't come with him. He had to stay on in Paris because of a dispute with Gaston Prémont, Cyrille Delannoit's manager. But the main reason for his absence was that he had decided he wouldn't have anything more to do with the Piaf–Cerdan liaison. On Wednesday 17th, Cerdan acted out his fight against Tony Zale on the stage of the Gaîté Lyrique before an audience of artistes charmingly dressed in costume, all lace and wigs. Roupp was in the audience. For the sake of appearances, he accompanied Marcel to Orly, telling anyone who wanted to hear: 'I'll be joining him soon.'

But Roupp's presence wasn't really missed in the apartment at 891 Park Avenue. Edith pressed Marcel with questions. And Marcel had so much to tell her. His triumphant return to Paris, Vincent Auriol, Casablanca, the *Bal des Petits Lits Blancs*, Cocteau, the dinner he gave one evening in the rue Leconte de Lisle:

'It was wonderful, Edith. I asked Emile to fetch Madame Barrier. It was a good move. There were about fifteen people that evening.' Edith kept asking him about the evening at the *Bal des Petits Lits Blancs*. 'You were right,' Marcel said. 'Your friend Jean Cocteau was wonderful to me. It was the greatest honour of my life. And, do you know, Roupp reproached me for it.'

'What! What's it got to do with him? What does Roupp know about it?' Edith had had enough of Roupp. And when Marcel told her that he was going to make a film, she was up in arms. 'What are you talking about?'

Marcel was embarrassed: 'It was in Casa. I was at home. I met someone from the Havas agency. And I signed.'

'What did you sign?'

'I won't know till later. They haven't got a title for the film yet. It's a film about my life.'

Edith was beside herself at such naivety. She grabbed his wrists: 'Marcel, Marcel! What have you gone and done? You're talking about a film without a name, without actors, director or screenplay. And how much have you been given?'

'I'm wrong, Edith, it has got a title. They did decide on one in the end. It's going to be called *The Man with Hands of Clay*. Roupp mentioned someone by the name of . . . Rivet and another person called . . . Mathot.'

Edith frowned. 'Marcel, this is dreadful. It's going to

156

be a rubbishy film. You must write to Roupp. We'll try and retrieve the situation.'

Marcel's letter was to haunt Roupp for a long time.*

'After discussing it at length with Edith, I have decided it would be disastrous for me to make a film with Léon Mathot. It would undoubtedly be absolute trash and the last thing I want is to look ridiculous, particularly in my first film.

'Edith knows some very good producers who are not just interested in box-office success but in making 'good' films. Edith knows all about the cinema and is quite categorical about Léon Mathot.

'I'd like you, as my supermanager, to find a way of getting out of this film or of getting it put off indefinitely so that I can make another one first which will bring in more money and enable us to shoot others. We are already in touch with a company which is ready to start as soon as we give them the go-ahead.'

Marcel may have signed the letter but as far as Roupp was concerned, Edith had dictated it.

Marcel went to the Versailles every evening with Edith. Nothing and no one could keep them apart, except for the exhibition bouts put on by Lew Burston and Sammy Ritchman. As Edith couldn't be with him during these bouts, she asked Loulou Barrier to go along. Marcel was never away for more than forty-eight hours at a time. After three short rounds he was back.

One Sunday, Marc Bonel expressed a desire to go and see the Niagara Falls. He envisaged himself filming the falls, considered to be one of the seven wonders of the

---

* Lucien Roupp, *Cerdan, La Vérité*, Presses de la Cité.

world. Bonel thought it would make a beautiful Sunday outing.

Edith soon put him straight. 'Well, you'll have to go without us! Don't imagine that we're going to go out of our way to see some water falling over a cliff.'

Bonel never got to see the Niagara Falls. But he and Marcel were treated to a proper visit to the Metropolitan, the biggest museum in New York. Jacques Bourgeat had told Edith to pay a visit. It was a must. Bonel was thrilled. He loved paintings so much that he visited all the museums in New York, at the rate of three a week. But they didn't manage to get through the grand masters at the Met. As usual, Edith's shoes were too small for her. She was very proud of the fact that her feet were size 35. Her toes were deformed. It looked as though every step she took was painful. Her feet often hurt her. This time it was particularly bad. 'Come on boys, my feet are killing me. Let's go home!'

Marcel did as he was told. He was completely caught up in the Piaf whirlwind. He let himself be carried along. The only thing that irritated him were Simone Berteaut's sudden changes of mood. Edith and Momone had frequent rows. The two sisters seemed to enjoy tormenting each other about their humble origins.

Marcel was always on his guard with Momone. He sensed the need to go carefully. For a start, Momone talked too much and too loudly. She also had a tendency to get things wrong and mix them up. And she drank. When she had been drinking there was no telling what she might do – including, as she had just threatened, revealing everything about Edith and Marcel.

'If you do that!' Edith screamed with clenched fists.

In a letter to Genevieve Lévitan, New York, 27 November 1948, Edith wrote:

'My dear Genevieve,

'I've got so much to tell you that it would take pages and pages to write. How much easier it will be to communicate in person, and how happy I will be to be able to unburden my heart to you. I know how understanding you are and I know you are a good friend!

'I don't need to tell you how happy I am at this moment . . . He is here and my life is complete!!!

'We are coming back on 20 December and I'll phone you as soon as I arrive.

'I can't really believe what's happening to me . . . I can't see enough of Marcel. I treasure every second and he's so marvellous that, the more I get to know him, the more I love him . . . I'm not putting it very well but these are the only words I can find to talk about him. I love him in a way I've never loved anyone else and I only have eyes for him!

'People are so disappointing. You can live along-side them, thinking they love you and then one fine day you realise that they really hate you – but *'ainsi va la vie'* ('that's life'), as Yves Montand would say. I had a friend I liked a lot and once again I realise that the friendship was all one-sided. It doesn't even make me sad any more. You get used to everything. Has this world no heart?

'Deep down, I don't care and right now I'm the happiest woman in the world!

'My heart is overflowing with happiness.
Love and kisses
Edith

P.S. My regards to your man. Mine sends his to you and yours.'

They were back in Paris on Thursday 16 December, at

dusk. They had wanted to make it a discreet, semi-secret homecoming. It wasn't to be. A photographer had been tipped off and came to get a picture. Edith saw him and tried to get out of it. She quickly turned her back. The photographer didn't get his scoop. But he did have a story . . . Once again, the names of Cerdan and Piaf appeared in all the papers and magazines.

In her column on Parisian life on page 2 of the *Parisien Libéré*, Jacqueline Michel alluded carefully to Edith and Marcel's affair:

> 'This is the second time Edith Piaf and Marcel Cerdan have flown home together,' she wrote. 'Edith has a reputation for liking tough guys, but she may not realise that people are beginning to talk . . .'

Ici Paris was less restrained, claiming that the return of the champion and the singer was straight out of the Wild West. Edith reportedly panicked at the sight of the photographer and cried out: 'Marcel, thump him!' The reporter was punched on the nose. If he remained in one piece it was because it was Longman, not Cerdan, who attacked him.

Edith had got to the point where she couldn't live without Marcel. The month they had spent as a couple had welded them together. They were now inseparable. It was Christmas 1948. Marcel felt obliged to go back to Marinette and his children, family and friends. Edith had the good fortune to land a contract in Casablanca. She would have to stay in hiding, but so what?

Marcel in Casablanca was quite something. The responsible, reserved boy in his neat grey suit was transformed into a carefree, relaxed individual in open-necked shirt and slacks. He was at ease here; Loulou Barrier and Marc

160

Bonel, whom he invited to visit his 'home country', saw this very clearly. He picked them up himself at their hotel in the Dodge he had bought in New York after his fight against Lavern Roach, and he drove them to Sidi Marouf, about ten kilometres outside town. This was where he had his farm. It was run by his brother-in-law, Narcisse Lopez. Barrier and Bonel were surprised to see Marcel take his role so seriously. He gathered his six employees, who included a liberated German prisoner who hadn't wanted to go home but had preferred to stay on and work for the Cerdans. Marcel had given him a job. He lived there with a local woman.

Marc Bonel got his camera out. He followed Marcel round as he asked after the animals, their food and the impending harvest of alfalfa, maize and oats. Bonel filmed it all. Later he showed the film to Edith. Marcel ended the tour by explaining the irrigation works in detail to Loulou. These had just been completed and would make his farm worth even more than the fifteen million it was valued at. Not a word was said about boxing.

They returned to town, driving down the boulevard de la Gare, past the Place de France, the casbah and, naturally, his bar in the boulevard de Lorraine. Marc got it all on film. It was the same smiling Cerdan everywhere, always surrounded by crowds of fans. He would stop good-naturedly for a photo, an autograph, or even a game of pétanque. This was the Cerdan you met in the streets of Casablanca, everyone's Cerdan. He was even mobbed by some conscripts who carried him triumphantly through the town.

Bonel went on filming until the evening. It only made Edith love him more than ever.

'No, Piaf didn't bring me bad luck.'

For Edith and Marcel, 1949 began with this announce-

161

ment. It was signed Cerdan and it made the headlines of *France-Dimanche* on 2 February. It was no declaration of love. How could it be? It was really a media operation mounted by the very people who had proclaimed the opposite seven months earlier. It was a coup, presented as a world exclusive.

It was Cerdan speaking:

'I'd been waiting for the opportunity for months. And then I got beaten by Delannoit. I hadn't put up my usual performance. We all fall prey to the occasional weakness. No one had any sympathy. I was attacked from all sides. When I saw the blazing headline: "Piaf Jinx on Cerdan", I was really furious. I would like to take this opportunity to set the record straight. I should like to make it clear that Piaf didn't bring me bad luck, because no one can bring bad luck to an honest man who does his job, and anyway I don't believe in "luck". On the contrary, I can honestly say that Piaf was invaluable to me at the toughest moment in my career . . . etc., etc.'

Then Marcel said how much he had always admired '*la môme* Piaf' who, through hard work and talent had become one of the greatest French performers. Marcel went further, without giving anything away about their romance:

'It was understandable that I should feel close to her when I saw her in the Club des Cinq. I smiled and blushed like a schoolboy when she spoke. However well-known he is, a sportsman always has a sort of complex when faced with a great star.'

He then went on to recapitulate the highlights of their

acquaintance. The day before his encounter with Abrams, he received an unexpected telegram which had deeply moved him. 'It was so simple that I couldn't get over it. I told myself you had to be amazingly subtle to be able to think up something like "Little Piaf sends a little piece of her heart" and that I would never have her intelligence. Later, after the fight against Raadik, which was a tough fight, she sent a comforting message, "a message which made me feel better".' Later still, after the fight he lost against Delannoit: 'I wanted to give it all up. She made me reconsider my decision.'

Marcel then concluded the article on a determined note:

'So you can see why I was unhappy when I read *France-Dimanche*. You must never judge people without taking all the background circumstances into account.

'The other day in New York I was dining with Monsieur Roussel, the director of Air France, when he quoted a phrase of Plato's. It's not my style to quote famous authors. If I mention it at all, it's simply because it made sense to me: "What I fear most is what people think of me."

'That's what I fear most. Because I feel I must do my duty. And my chief worry is that those who are close to me, and whom I love, should suffer, without cause.'

The year opened with this confession of love disguised as friendship. Two days later, there was a sensational divorce.

The rumour spread on Wednesday 4th that Cerdan was leaving Lucien Roupp. Felix Lévitan exploded the bomb in the *Parisien Libéré*. That day, Cerdan and Roupp had a meeting in the Club des Cinq. There was a tense exchange of words. For the time being what they had to say remained between themselves. But people noticed Roupp looked distraught as he left the club in Montmartre. Marcel made an off-the-cuff statement:

'It's over between Roupp and me. We're going our separate ways, but I want it to be a friendly break. I don't want the press to make a meal of it.'

The next day Marcel was forced to give an explanation. He said that it had all started with a conversation he had had on 24 December in Casablanca with Monsieur Laignaud, who had just set up a massive fruit-cake business in America. Although Cerdan was aware that the use of his name had been sold to advertise the cake firm, he didn't know that his manager was getting ten times more than him: 2,000,000 francs for the manager; 200,000 francs for the champion.

'There is no reason', Marcel had argued, 'for Roupp to do business on the side. This story opened my eyes. Besides, people tell me there's more to it than that.'

The switchboard at the Hotel Bergère in Paris, where Roupp was staying, was jammed throughout Thursday 5 January. The man who had been Cerdan's manager since 22 July 1937 (when Marcel was twenty-one) was besieged by all the papers of Paris, the rest of France and Morocco. Cold and unflinching, Roupp gave his version of the facts, the truth as he saw it:

'It was all triggered off by an apéritif,' he said. 'At the beginning of 1948 when we left for America, I entrusted Messieurs Carrière and Vallier with our commercial interests. I have since cancelled this power of attorney. While we were away my representatives did a deal with an apéritif company in Banyuls

164

for a lump sum of 500,000 francs. The company were to use Cerdan's name in their advertisements. When we returned to France I was thinking of using Cerdan's name to promote another product. When consulted, the Havas Agency informed me that the contract signed by my representatives required complete exclusivity for all food products, both liquid and solid. A few days later, the apéritif company released me from the contract on payment of 50,000 francs and on condition that I did a deal with Monsieur Laignaud, a cake manufacturer. So I negotiated with Laignaud: for an annual sum of 100,000 francs payable two years in advance he was to be able to use Cerdan's name until 1952. At the same time, I signed another contract linking myself directly with Laignaud, who agreed to pay me 25 centimes per cake sold.

'On 22 December I converted this private agreement, which was then destroyed, into a definitive contract under which Laignaud undertook to pay Lucien Roupp and Marcel Cerdan 55 centimes per cake, independently of the annual sum of 100,000 francs provided for in the first contract. In this way I managed to increase Marcel Cerdan's profit and it is over this profit that I made for him that my promising young athlete is attacking me today.'

Quite apart from the fact that Marcel could have got 25 centimes more per cake than the percentage he received, the world champion was demoralised by these revelations. He had no intention of taking Roupp to court. All he wanted to do was to free himself and forget their differences.

He instructed Jo Longman to defend his interests. Jo immediately wrote to Lucien Roupp asking for a copy of the contract which had tied him to Marcel since 18 April 1941. On that day Cerdan had effectively granted Roupp the right to sign for him in anything to do with fights, or his commercial and literary interests – for a period of ten years. In short, Cerdan was tied hand and foot. Although he had control over his autographs, he didn't have control over his signature.

From then on, Longman became Marcel's business advisor, in the same way that he had adopted a proprietorial interest in Cerdan's relationship with Piaf from the word go. Roupp had always been aware of the pact that existed between Longman and Piaf without understanding it. He had seen Jo's irritation at Edith's outspokenness, while she instinctively disliked Longman's shiftiness. But because of Marcel they managed to get along together.

For two days, the newspaper-sellers shouted themselves hoarse over the story. Many saw the mark of Piaf in the separation with Roupp. There was more than a grain of truth to it but it wasn't the whole story.

On Friday 6 January Marcel began a new life. For the first time since the world championship he went to the Bois de Boulogne in the morning to start running again. It wasn't far from the rue Leconte de Lisle to the Porte de Boulogne. Emile was only too happy to drive him there.

Sometime after twelve o'clock Emile would drop him off at the Epinay studios. Marcel hadn't been able to get out of the contract signed in Casablanca for the film *The Man with Hands of Clay*. But fortunately, Edith had intervened. She gave Marcel her instructions: 'No childish dialogue. Don't let them push you around. They have no right to present you with a *fait accompli*.'

As a result there were numerous changes and cuts in the original screenplay. Léon Mathot and Marcel Rivet were forced to meet all his demands.

Both actors and technicians were struck by Cerdan's extreme timidity when he arrived for the first day of shooting. Blanchette Brunoy, who played Marinette in the fictionalised biography, was disturbed by this charming creature, devoid of all pretence, who didn't like rehearsing in front of everyone. Marcel preferred to take refuge in his dressing-room, where he could really get into the skin of his own character. When Blanchette Brunoy brought her face close to his he would look away modestly. 'Don't look at me, it makes me embarrassed,' Marcel told her.

Fortunately, things sorted themselves out. Marcel felt his confidence grow as they got further into the film. In the end he even started to wish they hadn't had to dub his voice because of his Moroccan accent. 'If only I had a nice voice,' he told Blanchette Brunoy, 'I'm sure I could have made a career in the cinema.'

He was impressed by Léon Mathot's enormous patience and the indulgence of his fellow actors. Alfred Adam played Monsieur Lucien (Roupp), Philippe Hersent was Joe Marken (Longman) and Robert Berry was Postan, a character based on Victor Buttin, one of the three boxers to have beaten Marcel. On 15 August 1942, in Algiers, Buttin had won when Marcel was disqualified.

A young actor, this was Berry's third film. They had all been sports films. A former champion discus-thrower and shot-putter, this optimistic young man was at a loss to understand why the film parts he played always ended sadly. In *The Man with Hands of Clay*, he died following a training fight.

While they were shooting, he made a big effort every morning to shed some of his excess weight and to box properly – to learn to parry Cerdan's favourite blows and to collapse, simulating a blow below the belt.

Berry remembered that during a scene in *L'Idôle*, the

167

last boxing film shot in France, Montand had struck him such a blow on the skull that the staged fight had almost turned into a real battle. 'All in all, I prefer Cerdan to Yves Montand. At least Cerdan is accurate and doesn't hit me.'

Everyone who had played a part in Cerdan's life was included in the scenario, so it was only to be expected that Edith should appear in some guise.

Rivet and Mathot created a character who was both real and imaginary. They began by adapting the true story of Cerdan's encounter with the actress Simone Simon on board the *Ile de France* during Marcel's first transatlantic crossing. She was given the name Gabrielle Lucas in the film and was played by Marie-Thérèse Lebeau. She was a very famous fashion designer on her way to New York to present her winter collection.

The screenwriters were also inspired by the real-life story of the spontaneous collection organised by Marcel Cerdan and Simone Simon on board ship for the young stowaway who had given birth to a little girl. They included the event and the interpretation put on the story by a Parisian journalist. In the film an evening newspaper seized on the story and headlined it 'GABRIELLE LUCAS AND MARCEL CERDAN HAVE A CHILD ON BOARD THE ILE DE FRANCE.'

At this point, Gabrielle Lucas started looking more and more like Edith Piaf. She defied Monsieur Lucien just as Edith had stood up to Lucien Roupp. Like Edith, she organised her professional engagements to fit in with Marcel Cerdan's programme. Finally and above all, she was the involuntary heroine of a sensational press coup after the fight Marcel lost in Brussels against the Belgian Cyrille Delannoit – just like Edith. The paper was not *France-Dimanche* but *Je Dis Tout*. The headline read:

'GABRIELLE LUCAS KNOCKED OUT BY MARCEL CERDAN'S BLOW TO THE HEART' instead of 'PIAF JINX ON CERDAN'.

On his return from Brussels Marcel had a homecoming scene with his wife. Marcel Rivet set it in Paul's bar-restaurant in Montmartre.

Take 1: Followed by Monsieur Lucien, Marken and Postan, Marcel arrives at the rue d'Orsel. Monsieur and Madame Paul are serving customers at the bar.

'Where is Raymonde?' Marcel asks impatiently.

No one answers. Stunned by this cold reception, he stares at the owners of the bar in disbelief.

'Where is my wife?' he repeats, scowling.

'In her room,' mumbles Madame Paul, very reluctantly.

Cerdan hesitates, then runs to the stairs and clambers up two at a time. Raymonde is busy packing her suitcases. She turns round at the noise.

'Raymonde . . .' murmurs her husband affectionately.

She doesn't react and carries on packing. 'Ah,' she says calmly, 'it's you.'

Marcel comes nearer, pulls his wife towards him and tries to embrace her.

'I telephoned you from Brussels . . .'

Raymonde pulls away. 'I know.'

'Why didn't you answer?'

'Do you really want me to tell you?'

They are like two opponents challenging each other. All of a sudden, Marcel catches sight of a pile of open newspapers, including a crumpled-up copy of *Je Dis Tout*, with its cheeky photo of the champion laughing in the arms of Gabrielle Lucas. 'Oh. Is it because of the photo?'

Raymonde doesn't answer straight away. She

wants to spare his feelings. 'Listen, Marcel. I don't reproach you for anything. But I'm sure of one thing: I'm not the companion you need. Yes . . . Yes . . . You're an international star.'

Cerdan shakes his head. But his wife goes on: 'All I'm asking you is to let me go without shouting, to be kind, like a good friend.'

'Have you gone mad?'

'It's because I don't want to go mad that I'm leaving.'

'Don't you love me any more?'

She stares at him. 'I love you too much,' she says, unable to keep the passion out of her voice, 'to accept that you should not be mine alone.'

'Well then . . .'

'My mind's made up! I'm fed up with being on my own half the time! I've had enough of waiting up all night for your phone calls. I've had enough of trembling each time you're in a fight.'

'What about me?' asks Marcel, embracing her. 'Do you think I enjoy spending my life punching people and getting punched, living in boats, planes and trains?'

Raymonde extricates herself a second time from his arms. 'But you do find the time to impress Gabrielle Lucas!' she cries out, her voice breaking, bitterly jealous . . .'

Leaving the world of the cinema and re-entering the real world, Edith and Marcel were summoned to present themselves on Thursday 20 January at the commissariat (police station) in the rue Bassano in Paris (8th arrondissement). In association with the public prosecutor, a complaint had been lodged with the examining judge by

Mme Simone Berteaut-Maréchal against Marcel Cerdan and Edith Piaf, for illegal confinement.

Through her lawyer, Maître René Floriot, Momone stated that she had been 'beaten, tied up and illegally confined on 20 and 21 November in New York at 891 Park Avenue, then taken under escort to the airport'. She added that Cerdan then forced her to get on a plane for France.

Interrogated by Commissaire (Superintendent) Denis, Momone expanded on this straightforward factual explanation: 'I was having a violent argument with Marcel. He was frightened I would tell everyone that he and Edith were living together in New York. It would have been disastrous for him. He told me: "When you've been drinking you get things muddled up." Then he started hitting me. I tried to escape but he caught me and tied me up to prevent me leaving. Edith and Marcel kept me prisoner for five days. On 25 November they took me under guard to the airport and put me on a Constellation.' The next day, 21 January, around 9.30 p.m., Marcel, Jo Longman and Edith Piaf left the commissaire's office where they had been summoned to appear earlier in the day. Marcel was full of smiles. And the greatest surprise of all was that Simone Berteaut and Edith Piaf were arm in arm. Commissaire Divisionnaire (Chief Constable) Gillet and Commissaire Denis had managed to settle the dispute between Marcel, Edith and Momone by bringing them all together. Momone, who arrived shortly before 8.00 p.m. at the rue Bassano looked extremely tense and was sobbing as she climbed the stairs leading to office number 7 where Cerdan and Piaf were waiting for her. She ended up by going back on the statements she had made the day before. True to character, Momone had impulsively decided to take sides in the dispute between Cerdan and his ex-manager Lucien Roupp.

171

So ended the tragi-comedy which had been set in motion two months after the event, at the instigation of Lucien Roupp's cronies.

Edith had always been indulgent towards Momone. She forgave her again. She told Marcel, who was still upset about her attack: 'You mustn't be cross with her, you know. Momone is all that's left of my past. I have a deep affection for her. We met at the age of sixteen. We sang together in the streets.'

'It's still a bit much to take,' said Marcel, shaking his head.

'I know, you're right. But what can I say, I've always helped her get back on her feet again. She's my sister, you see. Her problem is that something gets into her from time to time.' (Edith and Simone were, in fact, half-sisters, but did not meet until their early teens.)

The reporters were more voracious than ever. Edith had to be convincing. She succeeded. Her tactic was to put off any questions about Cerdan and herself.

'What Simone told the police', she said with great aplomb, 'is completely absurd. That Marcel and I locked her up in New York? In other words, that Marcel and I were living together in New York? It's ridiculous. Can you imagine the scandal it would have caused in America after the world championship if we had been living together? According to her, Marcel boxed her. I really can't see Cerdan laying a right on Simone – Simone wouldn't have lived to tell the tale. It's true that she was living with me in New York. She was given her board and I paid her $90 a month. In addition, in Paris, my secretary, Solange, gave her 8,000 francs per month, which she handed over to her mother to bring up her daughter, Marcelle-Edith, Marcel's and my god-daughter. It is also true that she left New York after a horrible scene and that she was given a good slap – but it was I who

172

gave it to her. One evening, on my return home from the Versailles I found her blind drunk. And she had sworn to me that she had given up alcohol. At that point I just lost my temper. She obviously enjoyed waking the whole place up. Who, in my shoes, wouldn't have slapped her? So I organised her trip home and my manager, Loulou Barrier, took her to the airport. The "escort" that she referred to consisted of him alone.'

Like a shamefaced little girl, Simone wrote Edith a letter of apology:

'Edith, please forgive me. I know I'm in the wrong but it's been tough rising to the top and then sinking to the bottom again. When I was still a child, I spent the best years of my youth following you. I never thought twice about it or whether I might be hurting my parents. I stayed with you through thick and thin. The last thing I want to do is remind you of all that. I don't want to tarnish our memories of childhood, awful though it was in many ways. You have soared so high that I no longer have the guts to follow you, but wait a few months and you'll see: I'll turn over a new leaf. Edith, let's kiss and make up. That will give me the confidence I need.

Simone

'P.S. Tell me you still think of me as your little sister.'

When Marcel was questioned about this half-serious, half-ridiculous episode, his face lit up with a smile and he said disarmingly: 'The only person I fought in New York was Tony Zale!'

13

Clipped-Wings and a Broken Voice

Convincing as it was, Simone Berteaut's letter of apology could not make up for the damage done. All the American papers, even the *New York Times*, made the most of the whole business, to the detriment of Edith's career on Broadway and Marcel's position as world champion and a major US star.

Edith decided on a strategy which was partly genuine and partly an act. She let the press into her house in the rue Leconte de Lisle. She gave the same speech to all the journalists as though it were a text she had learned by heart. Dressed in grey flannel trousers and a pale blue top and wearing no make-up, she affected the look of suffering that was her usual stage expression. She looked like a woman who had been through a great deal. Her drooping eyebrows expressed both resignation and total weariness. People were struck by her pale but extraordinarily expressive face. She had serious words to say about Cerdan.

'I would not be able to sleep at night if I were to be responsible for tearing a man away from his children. I wouldn't be able to go on living. Yes, you can quote me on that. If I were to separate Marcel from his family I would kill myself . . . It is out of the question that the innocents in life should suffer. I know only too well what an unfortunate situation we're in. If Marcel were childless, it would all be much simpler: it would be one woman against another, fighting with the same weapons. But that isn't the case. I think I shall write to Marinette. She must be going through a terrible time and I don't believe that anything I could say would help. But I want her to know that the most important bond between Marcel and me is an exceptional friendship.'

Her face cleared. She went on: 'I've been at my wits' end these last few days. I went to see a medium. Forgive me, but I believe in these things. The medium's answer was very straightforward: "You can't stop seeing Marcel. You are an essential part of his life. If you were to abandon him suddenly, he would be lost. I would go further and say that you simply must be there in person at his next fights. As long as you're there, he'll win. The vibrations between you are good. You feel the fight so intensely that he unconsciously draws on your energy." '

Edith had been reassured. Before Cerdan, she had been Yves Montand's lucky mascot. He used to say that he carried Edith's soul on stage with him. Now the same thing was happening when Marcel went into the ring.

Edith and Marcel, 28 March 1949, Empress Hall, London
When Dick Turpin collapsed, blood spurted from his nostrils. Marcel's left hook had flashed out so fast that no one had seen it and no one could be certain whether it had hit Turpin's stomach before hitting his chin.

The fight had been organised by a furrier and a hat manufacturer in order to unseat a fish salesman who was Britain's main matchmaker at the time. But the twenty-one reporters from London who had been paid by the promoters to go all the way to Cerdan's training ground at Château Thierry came home declaring that Turpin would not survive more than four rounds. It was the

175

worst form of counter propaganda the fight could have received. The evening made a loss.

The first two rows of ringside seats couldn't be sold because they were so expensive (£10 each). In the end they had to be offered to the guests. There were women in evening dress, covered with jewels, and men in dinner jackets. Jacqueline, Jo Longman's girl-friend, Genevieve Lévitan and Edith Piaf sat side by side in the first row, forming a solid body of support for Marcel.

Marcel had not trained properly and had underestimated his opponent. He didn't give the same impression of concentration as he had in the past. But Jo Longman was very excited. It was his first fight as Marcel's corner man. When the bell went, it was he who received the midnight-blue robe which Marcel wore for the first time that evening.

Turpin was the archetype of a boxer who blocked all attacks. His blocking technique was disconcerting. Whenever Marcel tried to hit him, all he encountered were Turpin's arms and elbows.

Cerdan lost his cool. In the fifth round the audience hissed the world champion. Edith put her head in her hands; she didn't want to see or hear anything. Genevieve tried to reassure her: 'It'll be all right, Edith, don't worry.'

Until now the three friends had managed to keep their feelings under control. But as soon as Marcel stepped up the pace and hit out faster, they also let themselves get carried away. Edith became frenetic: 'Come on, Marcel. Faster! Faster!'

Then Turpin received the hook that counted.

An hour after his win, Marcel, Edith, Jo, Jacqueline, Felix and Genevieve Lévitan sat down to a cold meal in Cerdan's suite at the Mayfair: tongue of beef (tasteless), with salad (no dressing).

Marcel was thirsty. He ordered beer after beer. He had

a little graze on the right wing of his nose and another on the bridge.

His cheeks were flushed. He commented: 'Turpin didn't want to fight and I'm not surprised. The same thing's going to happen every time I fight in Europe. They're too suspicious. I prefer American boxers. At least they fight when they're in the ring. And do they fight! And perhaps I'm not as fast as I was.'

'Don't exaggerate, Marcel,' said Felix, who was trying to set his mind at rest.

'But it's true. I can't help it. It's my age. In the past when I found myself dealing with a faker, I could always find a way out. I would speed up. Now I have to be really warmed up.'

'Don't you think you're paying now for all the time you've been inactive?' said Felix.

Cerdan nodded. 'You're right. Six months without boxing is much too long. I'll never make the same mistake again. Besides, I just wasn't into it this evening. I said as much to Lew Burston before going into the ring. I wanted to sleep rather than fight. What is reassuring is that my fists didn't fail me, which is a good sign.'

Longman made everyone laugh over dessert by saying: 'My boy, I was pleased with you this evening and have decided to keep you in my stable . . .'

Later on, they went to the Palladium where the American Eleanor Powell was appearing. Fred Astaire's former dancing partner had become the top female tap-dancer. It was a fabulous show. Marcel was full of admiration. He joked: 'People praise my foot-work but it's nothing compared to hers!'

Genevieve Lévitan went further: 'What a dancer! What a magnificent body!' Marcel nodded his agreement.

Edith took Genevieve up on her remark. During the interval, when they were repairing their make-up in the cloakroom, Edith ticked her off: 'You shouldn't express such admiration for a woman in front of your husband. Be careful.'

Genevieve wasn't taken in. Edith wasn't alluding to Felix but to herself and Marcel. Genevieve had never seen her so possessive.

Edith and Marcel were once again separated for a few days. Piaf was opening at the ABC and Cerdan had gone off to Casablanca for a rest. Eight, ten, twelve days without him was too much for Edith. She decided that Ginou should make a day-return trip from Paris to Casablanca to exchange letters. She set up an effective but expensive and energy-draining system. 'Postmen are no better than anyone else. They can lose letters,' she said. Edith trusted no one but Ginou. She couldn't forget the day when something came over Momome and she stole their correspondence, jumped into a taxi and rushed off to sell it to the press. It had been a horrible experience.

Ever since then Edith, who felt a need to write to Marcel, sensing it brought him closer, had taken every possible precaution. Ginou met Marcel in the airport at the Cazes camp. Her instructions were to wait there until he had written a reply. Marcel used to write on the first piece of paper that came to hand, sometimes even on writing paper from his bar in the boulevard Gambetta, whose letterhead he took care to tear off. He signed himself Jules, in thick pencil. The first time Edith came across this signature she turned towards Ginou and asked her, 'Tell me, is Jules written with or without an "s"?'

Eventually, Marcel returned. It was a Thursday, 14 April. That afternoon, the Paris Racing Club was playing Lille in the Parc des Princes. He was friends with the Racing Club players, who included Ernest Vaast, Roger Quenolle and René Vignal. There were twenty-five thousand spectators. It was a superb match which was won 4–3 by the Racing Club. Marcel had to be there.

That evening he went to the ABC where the audience was literally hanging on Edith's every word. 'Encore! Encore!' they cried tirelessly. She ended her programme with her old hits. The show had been carefully compiled and included performances by the Compagnons and Tay-Run, an astounding acrobat. He would appear on top of a pole balancing a ball and two bottles of champagne neck to neck on his head. Jean Raymond presented a hilarious Faust performed by Tino Rossi, Montand, Bourvil and Charpin. Marcel reigned supreme in the wings. He was part of the décor. He had a circle of fans amongst the stagehands and walk-ons. One evening, for a gag, he sang along with the Compagnons, in his thin voice – all behind the curtain, of course . . .

Like all the men who figured in Edith's life, he always sported the Piaf regalia. You had to. They were all given a watch, a gold cigarette lighter, a pen, a cigarette-holder, and gold cufflinks by Boucheron or Cartier. Marcel put his foot down at the chain bracelet. He didn't think it would go down very well with the public.

As Ginette Richer (known as Ginou) recalls:

'I used to go shopping with Edith. We often went to Dominique France, in the rue Pierre Charron. It was a chic shop. Edith had shirts made to measure with embroidered initials. She would say, "Show me your ties." Club ties were in at the time. She would have them all out, and would stand back and choose. Sometimes we would spend over two hours there and leave with ten shirts, twenty-five ties, scarves, waistcoats and gloves. She loved pale blue. We never paid. Dominique France would send the bill straight to the rue Leconte de Lisle. Sometimes Marcel would come with us, but only very rarely, if he was going on to Dr Jurmand in the rue Marboeuf for a consultation about his hands. We didn't hang around long in the shop on those occasions. The funny thing was that Dominique France had a brother-in-law who was the spitting image of Marcel.

'Then Edith and I would go on to Morenzi's near the Place de la République to choose material for suits. Morenzi would panic when he saw us coming. Edith had a knack of getting him to undo all his rolls of cloth and of choosing the one right at the top of the shelves. We would then fix an appointment with Morenzi who would come to the flat to measure up.

'Underclothes were bought in other shops. By the dozen. We would hold them up to see whether they would fit. I can still hear Edith: "Do you think this will fit our boy?" Marcel wasn't very pleased about all this. The only things he was really happy to accept were the suits. He knew his own were old-fashioned, but he was clueless about prices.'

One of the highlights of the day in the rue Leconte de Lisle was Marcel's bath-time. Edith looked after him as though he were a child. She bought him little plastic toys. She liked splashing him and washing his hair. Sometimes, Ginou would help wash, rub and pumice him. Marcel was waited on hand and foot. During the afternoon they would spend hours lying by the record-player in the sitting-room.

One day Michel Emer dropped in on them. He found both of them very absorbed. They were listening to classical music. Edith had two favourite composers: Tchaikovsky and Beethoven. As though in Emer's honour, Marcel rose to his feet and carefully got out his favourite record: the Ninth Symphony. He put it on the turntable and folded his arms. The music filled the room. Then, in the middle of the piece, Marcel suddenly got up and set the arm of the record-player down at the beginning again.

'What are you doing?' cried Edith.

'There's a passage that I haven't properly understood,' replied Marcel, lost in concentration.

Edith cast a glance of pride and amusement at Emer. Emer couldn't get over it.

In the evening after the ABC, Edith and Marcel would go to the Ambassade de l'Opéra. It was a tiny restaurant, a bistro for artistes, with a row of tables, a long bench, a little bar and a room on the first floor which was hardly used. The people who frequented the restaurant preferred to squeeze in downstairs, even if it meant sitting on the stairs and balancing their plates on their knees. Those who couldn't get so much as the corner of a table or a step were served in their cars. There was an incredible hullaballoo. On occasion, the neighbours would throw down buckets of water, which cooled things off – for a bit.

Situated in the rue Sainte-Anne, the Ambassade de l'Opéra attracted all the night-owls. You would see Gabin, Chevalier, Colette Mars, Genevieve Guitry, Henri Bri . . . They would sit there telling stories and pulling each other's legs.

Every evening, Mado Fondo and her good friend Irene de Trébert slaved away, juggling with the plates. They managed to fit fifty place settings where there was space for twenty-five. They had set up the Ambassade just before Marcel won the title of world champion. Because he had won over the whole of France in the process, Marcel had become their guardian angel – and Edith their fairy godmother.

A photo of them taken by Harcourt decorated one of the walls. For Irene and Mado, it was a way of broadcasting the affair between the boxer and the singer. It was also a way of watching over it. It was in Irene and Mado's interest that Marcel and Edith's relationship should become public. Irene had understood everything, seen everything and experienced everything that first day in New York. On her return home, she told Mado: 'Do you want to hear the latest news? Marcel has got together with Edith. They're madly in love.'

At first, Mado thought it was a joke. She knew Marcel well. She had also spent time with Edith. 'Together, those two? It's impossible,' Mado told herself. As far as she was concerned, there was no way this could be more than a fleeting affair. First of all, it wasn't like Edith to live with a man for long. Secondly, Marcel, a good-looker, great boxer and a real gentleman, was always surrounded by women. His problem was that he had too many to choose from.

Irene had a hard job convincing Mado. 'I tell you, it's serious.'

'How strange life is,' was Mado's verdict. She conjured up pictures of Edith and Marcel on their own, as they had been when she met them before the war. Marcel had just arrived in Paris. At the time, Mado was running a hairdresser's at 66 rue de Provence. She was married to Francis Loubier who ran a restaurant called Le Cabanon in the rue La Bruyère. One evening a friend of her husband's, François Mercier, the former fullback of the Sète Football Club, then the top French club, came to dine at the Cabanon. He brought with him a young, glum-looking boxer with an emaciated face who didn't know what to do with his fists. He was shy – you practically had to force him to talk. It was Marcel.

It was the beginning of a close friendship. Marcel used to come to the rue de Provence every day. Mado grew fond of this big fellow who wanted to become boxing champion and was forever engaging in pillow-fights with her younger brother. He kept making her go to the cinema with them to see *The Three White Feathers*.

Mado had met Edith not long before, when she was with Raymond Asso, her 'légionnaire', and when she was known as Piafou. She sang at Gerny's. They all lived in the Bouquet de Montmartre in the Place des Abbesses. They were furnished rooms. Mado lived on the first floor. Piafou and Asso lived further up. They used to meet for meals in the studio belonging to the pianist, Pierre.

And now Edith and Marcel were together . . . How strange life could be!

Mado liked seeing them together. She could tell from Edith's eyes that she was passionately in love. And Marcel looked spellbound. Marcel was completely different when he was with Edith. He was chic, perhaps a bit constrained. Mado much preferred the Marcel they would see at lunchtime, when he would turn up on his own, with no warning, after his training, and rush down into the kitchen in the basement to seek out, and sometimes make himself, something to eat. She would cook him fresh pasta. He taught her to cook couscous.

As soon as he had swallowed the last mouthful, Marcel would kiss Mado and whisper to her in his boyish fashion: 'If you see Edith, don't tell her you've seen me.'

But there was no hiding himself at the Vélodrome d'Hiver. On Monday 25 April he was there in the front row, in one of the best seats, wearing a petrol-blue suit, white shirt, pocket handkerchief, socks and suede shoes. Everything looked new. Behind him were Gabin, Bernard Blier, Marcel Achard, Cocteau and Henri Contet. In the ring two boxers were shadow-boxing.

Berretrot, the official Master of Ceremonies introduced them: 'The two boxers were weighed this morning in the

183

offices of the newspaper *L'Equipe* . . . The American Steve Belloise . . .'

'That's him,' the crowd roared.

'Jean Stock . . .'

'There he is . . .' people shouted.

The organisers had gone all out that evening. Stock, the docker from Conflans-Sainte-Honorine, boxed the way he unloaded cement, with arched back, bow legs and flat feet. There were people in the audience who still had a vivid memory of his fight against Robert Charron. Charron had banged away with all his might for twelve rounds and Stock had tottered about and been tossed around, dazed and overwhelmed. He couldn't take any more when Charron finally let his guard down in disgust. Both Stock and the spectators took advantage of it to hit out. Charron was forced to give up in the fourteenth round.

But this evening Stock, known as the 'Anvil of the Ring', was faced with a different sort of client: Belloise, known as King Kong. The winner was supposed to fight Cerdan.

It was a big evening. The place was packed; there wasn't so much as a folding seat to spare. Seats had been sold on the black market. As soon as the fight started, Stock received a right and a cut opened above his eye. It was immediately obvious that they wouldn't go the distance. Belloise's arm shot out like a catapult. He advanced on the Frenchman and literally massacred him. It lasted eight rounds. It was pure slaughter.

When Belloise sent Stock to the floor with a tremendous right uppercut, a woman cried out, 'Stop it! Stop it!' The referee, Monsieur Simon, heard. And he stopped Belloise, as if he felt sorry for Stock.

Marcel was shattered by the fight. That evening he told Edith: 'I shouted, I egged Stock on. I shouldn't have. It's

184

criminal. People have no business encouraging two men to fight like that against each other for no reason.'

Once more, Marcel decided he had had enough of boxing. He wasn't the only one. The next day he read in the papers that Tony Zale had given up for good. And Belloise's name was put forward for the world championship. Marcel didn't comment. With good reason, as it turned out. Two days later there was an official telex declaring Jake La Motta the challenger. The fight was set for 22 June in Madison Square Garden, in New York.

Marcel had once seen La Motta fight Teddy Yarosz, the previous winter during his exhibition tour through the US. Recklessly, he had told Edith: 'You know, I could take him on without any training . . .'

Ever since he was a little kid, La Motta had been fighting and yelling and working and stealing and fighting. And getting beaten up by his old man. There were five kids. His father had never managed to land a steady job: he was Italian, and English just didn't come easy to him. They ended up in the Bronx.

When things went wrong, as they did all the time, La Motta Senior used to take it out on his family. It was always someone else's fault, never his own. Everyone got a taste of it. You couldn't say anything in front of him: he was always right and he would work off his anger by fighting. Jake suffered along with the others. He started to fight for money at the age of eight.

In the clubs in the Bronx, where guys went to booze and play cards if they had the money, the big game was to round up the local kids and throw coins to them. The kids would fight over who got the money. La Motta Senior got the picture. At least once a week he would take his son down to these places. Jake wasn't given a chance to say no. He had to earn his keep. The trouble was, once they got back to the house, the money went straight into their father's pockets. Once, at Christmas, Jake and his brothers hung up their stockings near the chimney. The next day they found a lump of coal in them. 'Santa Claus's punished you because you've been bad,' said the old man. There was no answer to that.

Brought up the tough way, Jake stayed tough. Having realised very early on that he had no choice in life but to steal or fight, he quickly decided to go in for real fighting after a brief attempt at real stealing: he learned how to box in the reform school in Coxsackie.

He soon became a good boxer, winning the diamond belt in the light heavyweight category. Most of his opponents were blacks, often weak with hunger. Jake took advantage of this; he boosted his record by fighting against no-hopers or worn-out old fighters, who were only too happy to earn some money to feed themselves.

Later on, he became one of the most promising middleweights in the country. He made the cover of *Ringside* magazine, of *The Ring*, and of *Corriere d'America*, the Italian-American newspaper. He was nicknamed the Bronx Bull. He defeated some of the best blacks in his category: Bert Lytell, Lloyd Marshall, Nate Bolden, Jimmy Edgar and Holman Williams. But they were just playthings in comparison with Sugar Ray Robinson. There was no love lost between these two. Robinson had won four out of their five fights, while La Motta firmly believed that his one victory was worth ten.

Then there were smears. Money was always at the root of it. Jake tired of fighting for prizes of $10,000 or $15,000, when he knew his mate Rocky (Graziano) made $150,000 by taking on Tony Zale. So when the boxing racketeers offered him $100,000 to throw a fight with Billy Fox, a black from Philadelphia, he may have sent them away the

186

first time on principle, but he ended up accepting the money.

The rigged fight took place on 14 November 1947. Fox boasted forty-three knock-outs, all, or nearly all, of which had been fixed. Normally, Jake would have massacred him with his first blow. But it was he who fell in the fourth round. Crouched against the ropes, he let the blows rain down. It was declared a technical KO. The spectators in the Garden were appalled and yelled out: 'Fake! Fake!' It was so obviously put on that the next day Dan Parker suggested in the *Mirror* that Actors Equity should complain about unfair competition!

La Motta was fined $1,000 and suspended for seven months in the State of New York. As soon as this period came to an end, he fought Ken Stribling in Washington and knocked him out in the fifth round. He won four more victories to improve his image before being beaten in Montreal by the Frenchmen Laurent Dauthuille, who opened a cut over La Motta's eye. La Motta got his revenge on Robert Villemain, whom he beat on points. But there was an after-taste of scandal about this revenge. Jake was almost beaten although he was declared the winner. Two days later, the judges responsible for this unfair decision had their licences revoked. La Motta was still regarded as an undesirable by Colonel Eagen when the NBA chose him as Cerdan's challenger. It was out of the question for the fight to be held in Madison Square Garden or anywhere in New York. He had got himself labelled for good. There would always be suspicions about him.

The fight was to take place on 16 June in Detroit. Detroit was Jake's territory: he had won fourteen out of the fifteen fights he had fought there. Only Robinson had beaten him.

Marcel took off from Orly on 19 May. He stayed at the Algonquin, the rendezvous of New York intellectuals. All the great minds came here. On the 22nd he was at Loch Sheldrake. He settled into his old pattern. The Evans family welcomed him like a prodigal champion. The same warmth was extended to his entire entourage: Jo Longman, Armand Cerdan and Roger Oquinarenne, manager of Annaloro and Yanek Walczak. The latter were to be on the programme at Detroit with Marcel.

Down by the lake a sign read: *Marcel Cerdan Bridge*. Marcel appreciated all this attention. When he spoke to Edith on the phone he told her how marvellous everything was, and mentioned all the little touches.

'And how's your voice?' he asked her, concerned.

'Don't worry. It's much better. I want to hear about you.'

A terrible thing had happened to Edith at the ABC over a month ago. She had developed a sore throat which she was unable to shake off. She had been forced to leave the theatre at short notice. There were serious suggestions that the great 'chanteuse réaliste' had lost her voice for good.

Edith decided that she was going to prove them all wrong. She took the first contract which came up. She agreed to sing for a fortnight at the Copacabana, formerly the Beaulieu. In her defiance she even sang two new songs: *'La petite Marie'* written by Edith and composed by Marguerite Monnot, and *'Les amoureux chantent'*, a poem by Jean Jeppy, also put to music by Marguerite Monnot.

Jean Jeppy was an unknown. He was twenty-two. Piaf decided to make him famous in a fortnight.

Marcel was reassured. Everything was all right with his little Edith. She wasn't about to be dethroned.

They spoke at length every evening on the phone. Neither of them wanted to be the first to hang up. Marcel had been gone a fortnight. From the start, his life at Loch

Sheldrake was less demanding than on his previous visit. He discovered the drive-in cinema. He thought it was marvellous. He wanted to open one in Casablanca. He paid frequent visits to farms in the area – potential models for his farm at Sidi Marouf. He and Walczak went shopping like housewives and argued over prices for the sake of it. He helped unload a lorry of food products to please Rhoda Evans, Jacky's wife. And if Walczak was the polka king (he had to be), Marcel won first prize in a tango contest.

In Paris, the newspapers soon started raising doubts as to the seriousness of Cerdan's training.

At the end of the line he would hear Edith's anxious voice: 'Marcel, it isn't true what I've been reading, is it?'

'What have you been reading?'

'They say you've been training like a circus kid.'

'Who wrote that?' asked Marcel.

'Robert Bré in *Paris-Presse*.'

'Don't believe a word of it . . . I swear I've never worked as hard.'

'You really swear it?'

'I swear it!'

When he got to Detroit ten days before the fight, Marcel was back on top. He moved into a suite in the Wittler Palace. Longman created a little bit of France on the sixth floor of the hotel, handing over as cook to Walczak, a first-class chef.

In the morning Cerdan jogged, in the afternoon he did gymnastics, and in the evening he played jacquet, or read a few pages of *Via Mala* by John Knittel or *Hatter's Castle* by Cronin, and got plenty of rest. Marcel's face had thinned out, in contrast to when he had taken on Dick Turpin in London, three months earlier. Marcel was in shape. You could see it and sense it.

As Yanek Walczak says:

189

'I was in a better position than anyone to assess Marcel! I was the one on the receiving end of his blows and I tell you, if he hadn't been a great companion and if I hadn't been aware of how much he had at stake, I'd have said: "That's it. I've had enough. Let someone else have a go." I was running out of steam. It was all I could do to survive three rounds in the training sessions. I don't mind admitting it.

'At the beginning everything was fine. I was further advanced than Marcel in my training, but as time passed in Loch Sheldrake and Detroit, Cerdan's shape improved and my ribs began to suffer. I have come across some tough people in my life, especially in the mines, but I'd never seen anyone as tough as he was then.

'I was lucky enough to have seen La Motta box. I knew what he was like. He was a difficult customer, always on the look-out for a scrap. Well, that's what he was in line for! I always maintained that he wouldn't last ten rounds before collapsing under Marcel's body blows.

'With big gloves on, Marcel would knock the breath out of me without even trying. He was usually very careful. Imagine what it was going to be like in the ring! La Motta could do what he liked, but Marcel's left hook had never packed so much punch. As his sparring partner I can tell you he really thrashed.

'Cerdan was on form. He had natural strength. And what strength! I couldn't get over it. His lungs were in good shape and his legs were everything they should be. Every evening I used to pray that Marcel would decide not to put his gloves on the next day, or that he would only do one or two rounds, instead of three – not three please, because it hurt so much!'

The night before the fight, Armand Cerdan, who was sharing a bedroom with his brother, heard him tossing and turning all night long. Armand didn't sleep a wink. He knew that Marcel wouldn't be able to relax until he heard the bell. Before turning in, the two brothers had talked about La Motta's style.

Marcel was dismissive. 'So what? Everyone keeps telling me how strong he is, that he knows how to fight and that I will back down. We'll soon see how strong he really is.'

Armand smiled. 'Take it easy, Marcel. Don't get yourself all worked up. There's no point. Forget about the spectators. Just think about your title. Don't get into a brawl with him.'

'But Armand, I'm strong enough to win a brawl. I'm as strong as I was when I fought Zale.'

Marcel, 16 June 1949, Briggs Stadium, Detroit

It was a big grey building. It loomed up austere and imposing in the heart of the motor city. The ring had been set up in the middle of the grass. There were twenty-five thousand spectators. At 9.00 p.m. La Motta slipped between the ropes, cloaked in his famous robe of fake leopard skin. It was all part of the act. They were waiting for Cerdan. La Motta took the opportunity to warm up with some shadow-boxing in his corner, but it was only a short respite.

Marcel arrived a minute later. He stepped forward to shake La Motta's hand, but La Motta ignored him disdainfully and went on shadow-boxing. There was a great roar of applause for Cerdan. La Motta also got a noisy reception but half of it was boos.

La Motta started by throwing a one-two at Cerdan's jaw. Cerdan delivered a left hook. La Motta moved back in with his head down. It descended into a free-for-all.

191

There was a left jab from La Motta followed by a left hook to the body. La Motta doubled and tripled his left hooks to Cerdan's face. He boxed with extraordinary speed.

Cerdan had a small cut on the corner of his nose and above his right eye. La Motta delivered a new series of hooks with both hands. Cerdan crouched against the ropes. He was clearly shaken. It was obvious to everyone that La Motta had the upper hand. Marcel slipped and fell. It was the classic lucky punch. But he was on his feet again immediately. He was taking punch after punch. La Motta's round.

Second round: La Motta took a violent hook in his face. Cerdan's round.

Third round: Cerdan couldn't keep him off. Advantage La Motta.

Fourth round: Cerdan couldn't use his left any more. His shoulder hurt. La Motta's round.

Fifth round: Stalemate. Cerdan was given a massage during the break.

Sixth round: With the use of only one arm Cerdan couldn't fend off La Motta any more. La Motta's round.

At the end of this round, Lew Burston sent the American second George Ranter to look for a painkilling swab. Ranter left the stadium and went twenty-five blocks before finding a drugstore that was open. It was too late . . .

Seventh round: Cerdan's left arm now gave up completely. Marcel received jab after jab without even trying to block them. La Motta's round.

Eighth round: Burston and Longman wanted to call a halt. Marcel whispered to them: 'If you stop the fight I will kill myself!' La Motta was now trying to land the big one. La Motta's round.

Ninth round: Cerdan had now given up all hope. La Motta delivered a string of lefts followed by a string of rights. Marcel staggered about and hung onto his opponent. Blows rained down on him. His face hurt. La Motta's round.

Tenth round: Marcel threw his head back. He remained seated on his stool. Burston called the doctor into the ring. The referee stopped the fight.

La Motta had become world champion.

14

Jake, Rocky, Frankie and the Others . . .

'Fifty thousand bucks! . . . Don't worry ducks.'

Jake played the part, patting the big gold buckle on his world championship belt studded with diamonds and rubies. He strutted about in front of his wife, Vickie, a magnificent pin-up blonde, straight out of a magazine, and repeated, arrogantly: '$50,000, don't worry about me, buddies.'

He was addressing the 'gentlemen' who made up his circle. These 'gentlemen' were also of Italian origin. They had their headquarters in the Book Cadillac Hotel. Their leader was Frankie Carbo. He drove around in a black Cadillac and never went anywhere without his bodyguards who looked like something out of *Scarface*. He was a familiar figure in the New York fruit-machine world. He had an affable smile, wavy white hair and a quick, piercing gaze. He dressed soberly and elegantly, usually wearing a pale suit. He was said to apologise before shooting people.

He seemed to have led a charmed life. He was given the nickname 'God the Father of boxers'. He had won a lot of money by taking bets on La Motta's opponents. He had boxing and gambling contacts throughout the US. Known as the most skilful manipulator in the history of boxing, he was a past master at the art of playing the odds.

All these 'gentlemen' were taking enormous numbers of bets. Generally, when La Motta's opponent was backed as the favourite, La Motta won, but sometimes when La Motta was very heavily backed, he lost. As luck can sometimes be stubborn, these 'gentlemen' would help it along a little. In any case, Jake and his old friend Rocky (Graziano) were under contract to Carbo. It was he and he alone who decided. If Jake was walking around swaying his shoulders and showing off his fine $50,000 belt, it was all thanks to the boss.

Jake was quite open about it. He had been in the garden of his house in the Bronx playing with his dog when Joey, his brother, had suddenly turned up, all excitement.

'Hi, champ!'

Taken aback, Jake almost hit him. 'Don't piss me around.'

'No, I'm serious,' Joey insisted. 'I was in the gym when the boss called. Yes, the boss himself. He told me: "When Jake's period of suspension is over, he can have a go at the title. It's his turn." '

Jake threw himself at Joey. Things became a bit more complicated later on when Jake found out that he would have to stump up $20,000 in cash before the match. But Jake couldn't back out, so he hit on a brilliant idea. As Cerdan's challenger he would only get a purse of $19,000 . . . He very nearly had to pay out of his own pocket. He scraped around. He had $10,000 left. He put it on himself at 8–5. He picked up $16,000. Jake was no fool.

Marcel was in the depths of despair. He had lost the title he had fought so hard to win and to a decidedly dubious opponent in a decidedly dubious atmosphere. This alone was enough to depress him. But there was something else. His injury, for example, remained mysterious. A few minutes after the end of the fight, Dr Vincent Nardiello, the official doctor attached to the New York Boxing Commission, diagnosed a tear or supraspinatus strain of the elevator muscle probably with a haemorrhage. The next day in New York the same doctor took an X-ray of Cerdan's shoulder in Saint Clare's hospital. He announced shortly afterwards that the X-ray showed absolutely nothing. Another official doctor, Dr Joseph Cahallan, examined Cerdan. He came to the same conclusion: there was no external sign of injury.

And now, to make matters worse, the sports journalists were raising questions both about Cerdan's training and Lew Burston's overconfidence before the fight. And why did Marcel agree to go into the ring immediately after a game of jacquet when he was suddenly informed that the fight had been brought forward? Significantly, La Motta had spent the previous half-hour shadow-boxing to warm himself up. Were these simply mistakes or were they signs of negligence?

When Loulou Barrier met Marcel at Saint-Lazare station he hardly recognised him. Marcel immediately asked him how Edith had taken it.

'She's waiting for you,' Barrier replied. 'She's completely demoralised.'

Edith was in a state, angry at herself for not having gone over to the States. 'Marcel,' she said, 'I should have been there with you.'

'Do you think so?'

'Of course! But I'm never going to leave you again. And we're going to get out of here. I'm fed up with this house. It feels sad.'

'Do you think so?' He would have gone along with anything she said.

A few days later they bid goodbye to Auteuil and moved out, lock, stock and barrel. Edith had found a magnificent house on the edge of the Bois de Boulogne, at 5 rue Gambetta. There were rooms everywhere, columns, a spiral staircase, terraces, a bathroom in pink marble, attics, basements and a large room destined for Marcel's training.

When she was shown round, Edith immediately concluded that the man who built the house must have been mad. His name appeared on the façade: Emilio Terri. He had made a bet in the thirties that he would build the largest possible building on the tiniest plot in the neighbourhood.

Edith soon imposed her own inspired chaos. It was as though a theatre set were being assembled instinctively, any old how, yet with a sense of conviction. It was like living out of a suitcase. But in the midst of this flurry of furniture, American goods, fur coats and plants, Edith maintained a sanctuary for herself, a few square feet of peace. It was her room – their room. It was dominated by a white piano and the latest model of TV set. There were pictures by primitive artists on the walls, not a modern picture to be seen.

'One day,' she said to Marcel, 'we'll buy ourselves a Rembrandt and a Corot.'

'Oh yes, why?' asked Marcel.

'Because they're really good painters.'

Marcel went off to Rome. He was bound by the terms of his contract to make a second film, *Al diavolo la celebrita!* (To Hell with Fame!) There was no way he could get out of it. Edith's view was to hell with obligations. But boxing films were all the rage at the time. The Americans had a stock of them. They had just released *The Champion* with Kirk Douglas, and were already announcing another boxing film with Robert Ryan. The prospect of earning a few million francs dispelled whatever doubts Marcel might have had about signing. There was no point in looking a gift-horse in the mouth, even if the plot did end badly for Marcel: he was to die at the end, following a car accident.

Edith and Marcel met up three weeks later in mid-August in Cannes. She was in the middle of a summer tour. It seemed as though they hadn't seen each other for close on a century. They discovered each other all over again. Her movements were delicate. He became bashful. Afterwards, she laughed till she cried listening to him telling stories about the shooting of the film.

'No, it can't be true, Marcel. You didn't really, did you?'

'I did, I swear, but it wasn't on purpose.'

'But what did the director say?'

'He said it was very good and that on no account was the scene to be altered in any way.'

Marcel had been explaining to Edith how, in the middle of shooting, he had pulled off an amazing KO which wasn't in the script. The victim was an Italian by the name of Fernando Janilli, a real boxer. 'Let's have a real fight,' Marcel had said to the Italian. In the heat of the moment he delivered a left hook and put Janilli right out of the game.

'Was he cross with you afterwards?' asked Edith who couldn't contain her laughter.

'No, he was a good guy, but what got him was that the sequence is to stay in the film.'

Edith thought Marcel looked superb, positively radiant. His suntan suited him. 'How handsome you are Marcel,' she kept telling him, fluttering her eyelashes at him . . .

Jo Longman soon caught up with them. He had received a cable from Lew Burston telling him to get ready: La Motta and his 'gentlemen' had decided to offer Cerdan his return bout without delay. The fight was planned for 28 September in the Polo Grounds in New York.

'Wonderful!' cried Edith. 'This time, I'll be there with you.' She had just signed a new five-month contract with the Versailles where she was to open on 15 September.

Marcel turned to Jo: 'When do you want to go?'

'As soon as possible,' replied Jo somewhat impatiently. 'It's time we shut them up.'

'What do you mean?' asked Edith.

'Lew's got me a bit worried, ' said Longman in embarrassment. 'There are all sorts of strange rumours going round over there. People are claiming Marcel let himself be bought or that he gambled on La Motta. Bullshit like that. But they're serious charges.'

There was a silence. Marcel was disgusted. 'How can people say things like that! They're going to pay for it!'

To take his mind off it, Edith took him out to Juan-les-Pins in the evening. She was singing. There was a festival with fireworks. Marcel agreed to give the starting signal for a race of home-trainers. They made him ride a bicycle. He didn't have it in him to refuse. The audience of holidaymakers made him feel warm inside. They treated him as if he had already regained his crown. He swore to himself he would.

They hadn't stopped kidding around since the plane had taken off. Edith was bubbling over with excitement. Genevieve Lévitan, who was going with her and was beginning to get used to her, let herself be caught up in this exuberance. It was always the same when Marcel was waiting for her at the end of the journey.

He had left a fortnight earlier on the *Ile de France* with Jo and Paul Genser. They stayed two days in New York and then went 'home', as he put it, to Loch Sheldrake.

Edith could picture it. A year already since she was last

199

there! She nudged Genevieve. 'Wait until you see how nice it is. You're going to like it.'

Although she had never seen it, Genevieve knew all there was to know about Loch Sheldrake and its environs. She could imagine the kind of life she would lead there. She and Edith were to be together day and night in the same bungalow, right next to Marcel's. It had been reserved in the name of Mme Lévitan. They were going to have to resort to various ruses, cover their tracks, and play cops and robbers. It might be amusing but it was more than a bit dangerous. Genevieve told Edith: 'I do hope you two are going to be careful. Think of Felix. You mustn't put him in a difficult position *vis à vis* the other journalists.'

'Don't worry about your husband, sweetie. Nothing can happen to him. Marcel and I aren't crazy.' Tears appeared in Edith's eyes whenever she mentioned his name. Deep down, there's nothing like a secret affair. She liked thinking of their first stay in Loch Sheldrake; Cerdan in the limelight and Piaf hidden away waiting for him.

A hostess leaned over to serve them an appetising meal. She was very attentive and kept calling them 'Madame'. Edith suddenly came to. 'What do you think you're doing?'

The hostess hesitated briefly. 'I was going to serve you, Madame.'

Genevieve couldn't stop herself from smiling. 'Don't worry, my friend's not all here at the moment.'

'What on earth do you mean?' Edith flared up.

'Nothing,' said Genevieve. 'Nothing.'

'No, go on tell me,' said Edith.

'Nothing, eat up.'

'What, eat this? You must be joking.'

'But it looks good,' protested Genevieve.

'No, it's not. These things travel backwards and

forwards. You don't know where they've come from,' Edith exclaimed. 'You don't know what's in this.'

'Don't be silly. There's nothing wrong with it.' Genevieve stood up for herself.

'Maybe, but we're not having any!' And Edith took some sandwiches that her Chinese cook Chang had prepared for her out of a plastic bag. 'Let's eat this, it's safer.'

Genevieve didn't argue. There was no point in protesting. If you wanted to be Edith's friend you had to go along with her tastes and demands.

Genevieve Lévitan says:

'Edith was like that. If you were hungry when she didn't want to eat, she called you piggish. You had to sleep when she wanted to and drink when she was thirsty.

'In New York I spent every moment of the day and night with her. That was when I saw the real Edith. Every evening there would be five or six of us for dinner, including Bonel, Chauvigny and Barrier. Edith had two French cooks. The first evening she asked me if I liked chicken and rice. I liked it well enough but I never imagined I would be eating it every meal. After a week I got tired of chicken and rice. I went to the kitchen and asked them to cook me a steak. When the steak appeared on the table, Edith cried out in horror: "Who's that for?" I thought she was joking and helped myself. Edith burst into tears. I didn't understand. I was embarrassed. She asked me in a distraught voice, "Don't you like my chicken and rice?"

'Edith was much less capricious at Loch Sheldrake. She wasn't in control of events there. Otherwise it was as I had been told, except that . . . how shall I put it? . . . Let's say I was worried I would be in the way when Marcel came over to be with Edith. But I was immediately put at ease. He came to our bungalow every evening at nightfall. He would stay for an hour or two, depending on how tired he was. We played cards. He cheated and we would catch him in the act. He laughed and we laughed. There was a magical atmosphere. Edith acted kittenish, but Marcel deliberately avoided any physical contact. From time to time she would glance at me as if to say: "Are you going to leave us in peace or aren't you?"

'We didn't stay long at Loch Sheldrake. Edith had to rehearse for her new show at the Versailles. We went back to New York. Edith no longer had the apartment on Park Avenue. She had found another bigger one on Lexington Avenue, at 136 East, on the corner of 67th Street, a stone's throw from Central Park.

'Every lunchtime we would go for a walk in the Park. She would go out in trousers and a sweater with a scarf to hide her curlers. We always went the same way: Lexington Avenue, Park Avenue, Fifth Avenue. We counted the streets by blocks. After two blocks, we turned right . . . after another two blocks we turned left. When we got to Central Park, Edith always went in through the same gate, the one on the left. Sometimes, I would make a surreptitious effort to go another way, take the third block or the gate on the right . . . to no avail. She liked keeping to the same pattern. She was superstitious. She always talked about the same things: her profession, literature, Marcel, Marcel, Marcel. She dreamed of going away with him and his three children. She was quite out of touch with reality. She thought that one day she would have him all to herself.'

202

One evening, after speaking to Marcel on the phone, Edith found she couldn't go to sleep. Late at night, wearing rollers and a hair-net she crept into Genevieve's room. She looked at Genevieve to see whether she was sleeping and when she found she was, Edith tapped her on the shoulder and asked innocently: 'Oh, were you asleep? What a shame, I came to sing you something.'

Genevieve didn't bat an eyelid. She pretended to be fast asleep. A few seconds went by. Genevieve wondered what was going through Edith's mind. Then it became clear. Edith began by singing to herself. Then her voice grew louder. Genevieve's eyelids trembled. It was one of Damia's songs *'Les Goélands'*. Edith wanted to sing Damia's entire repertory. Genevieve stretched out an arm to turn on her bedside light. It stayed on till early morning . . .

The Versailles gave Piaf a royal welcome on 15 September. She opened to the most select audience ever gathered for a Manhattan première. People were pointing each other out in the auditorium: Cary Grant, Gary Cooper, Rex Harrison, Lily Palmer, Barbara Stanwyck, Eliott Roosevelt, Claudette Colbert, Mr and Mrs Henry Ford and the French Ambassador, Henri Bonnet.

Edith had chosen eight songs for her programme. They included four which the Americans adored: *'L'accordéoniste'*, *'Le fanion de la Légion'*, *'La vie en rose'* and *'Monsieur Saint-Pierre'*. There was also an unpublished song called *'Hymne à l'amour'*. Marguerite Monnot had composed the music but Edith had written the words, which were inspired by her romance. 'It's beautiful because it's about Marcel and me,' Edith liked to tell people who were in the know.

Marcel was like a lion in its cage that evening at Loch Sheldrake. He had polished off three games of jacquet with Jo and Paul. He went to bed, gloomy and frustrated at having missed Edith's première. He was cross with himself. The next day he decided to go to New York and be back the same day. A few scenes on television decided it for him. It might seem completely crazy to neglect his duties as champion even for a day but it was stronger than him. It was fruitless trying to stop him, he was so determined. He had seen her for five minutes on television. There were two Ediths on the screen: a full-length view of her standing on the stage at the Versailles, and a head-and-shoulders shot. He had never loved her so much. Longman didn't try to reason with him. He let him get into Jo Rizzo's car, but he did manage to get Cerdan to promise to be back that evening.

Now Marcel was praying that his left shoulder was 'shock-proof'. That was the only remaining problem. For the last five weeks there had been a trail of American reporters to the Evans Hotel. They studied every training session, scrutinised every movement Cerdan made. A week before the world championship Marcel looked all set to win. Rex Smith of the *Herald Tribune* was the most impressed: 'La Motta may be world champion, but he only beat Cerdan's shadow. This time round, Jake won't be able to stand up to him.'

The sight of him landing blows and pounding the sandbag with his left destroyed any remaining doubts about the recovery of Marcel's shoulder.

For the past month he had been getting up at eight. Ten minutes later he was on the tennis court playing Roger Oquinarenne and Jo Longman who were well-matched opponents. He jumped, ran and sweated for an hour. He would then return to his bungalow to lie down. His afternoon work-out was organised by the trio Longman, Burston, Willy Ketchum; the latter was one of the greatest boxing experts in the United States, and a nice guy with it.

Marcel used to leave his things lying about. Willy commented to him on this and ended up paying out of his own pocket for a case which locked. Marcel was taken aback by his kindness. Later on, Cerdan left him a present of $500 which prompted the following comment by Willy: 'I've been in the boxing world for thirty years. He's the first person who's ever thanked me. Marcel could have treated me in a high and mighty way. But he didn't. He always listened to me and respected me the way a child of sixteen looks up to a teacher.'

In addition to Walczak and Annaloro, who were again on the bill at the Polo Grounds, Ketchum selected the light heavyweight Tony Betucchi and the middleweight Vic Costa to train Marcel. These two sturdy young New Yorkers had been instructed not to spare La Motta's challenger. By the time he stepped over the ropes in the Polo Grounds, Marcel's fists and legs would have done seventy rounds.

On Saturday 24 September he was on peak form. He had slept flat out for twelve hours solid. His face radiated serenity. He strolled through the corridors of the Evans hotel holding a book by Arthur Koestler, the latest Edith had recommended to him.

The phone went at lunchtime. Longman picked it up. It was Burston calling from New York.

'Something terrible's happened. La Motta's stopped his training. He's pulled out.'

Longman flew into a rage. 'What d'you mean?'

'Its true, Jo,' Burston told him. 'I've got the communiqué in front of me. It's official. Apparently, La Motta has hurt his right shoulder. It happened on Thursday during his training session.'

'Do you believe it, Lew?' asked Longman.

'Not for a minute. But there's nothing we can do about it . . . Tell Marcel.'

The news destroyed Marcel. It was a long time before he could bring himself to speak. His whole world had collapsed.

He phoned Edith. When she had got over the shock, she reacted well. He listened and began slowly to recover. She didn't make any fancy speeches but just kept talking. 'You'll have your revenge, you'll have it in good time.'

'Two years,' Marcel told her, 'I'll box for another two years, if I have to!'

'Come here. I'm waiting for you.'

Edith let Marcel hang up.

La Motta's withdrawal cost the organisers $70,000. But Jake was the real loser. He had turned the whole of America against him. The next day all the papers launched into La Motta.

In *The American*, Burston wrote: 'It's put on! We have no proof that he's hurt himself. We don't even know whether it's his shoulder or the nape of his neck . . . you've got to laugh.'

Dr Vincent Nardiello, who had confirmed Marcel's injury in Detroit went further: 'Jake is lying!' he stated during an improvised press conference.

Lester Bromberg was categorical in the *World Telegram*: 'Cerdan would have won easily on points.'

Finally, Lewis Burton, a scathing writer, spelled out in black and white what everyone was saying more or less out loud: 'This is just a manoeuvre to protect those of his friends who had put money on him . . . just before Cerdan shows everyone what wonderful shape he's in.' Lewis Burton didn't go so far as to reveal the name of the person who had triggered it all off, but everyone, beginning with Marcel, had a very good idea whom he had in mind: Rocky Graziano.

Two days before Jake pulled out, Rocky had been to Loch Sheldrake to pay a courtesy call on Marcel. At least, that was what everyone thought it was. As soon as he arrived at the Evans Hotel, Rocky had dismissively informed all and sundry that his pal Jake would win.

Jake and Rocky had been two of a kind since childhood. As kids they had battled with each other in the Lower East Side. They were made for each other, made to pull jobs off together. They used to have a running gag: they only stole things beginning with an 'a': a car, a watch, a radio. They ended up getting nicked. Rocky was the first to fall into the hands of the cops. He was thrown inside and locked up in the reform school at Coxsackie, where Jake soon joined him.

Their reunion on the inside sealed a bond between them. The screws would never forget it. Jake had just been sent down for three years. He was bawling everyone out, causing trouble and insulting the screws when his face suddenly lit up with a bit smile. He had recognised Rocky's voice behind him: 'Hey, Jake. It's you! Bullhead!'

Jake turned round and thumped Rocky in the ribs. 'God, it's good to see a friendly face around here!'

So Rocky was sure his buddy Jake was going to win, but when Cerdan really hammered away for five rounds, Rocky said to himself people would smell trouble. For show and publicity, he congratulated Marcel in front of the photographers.

What happened next? When your name is Rocky and you are like a brother to Jake, and the godfather of your family is called Frankie Carbo, you repay old debts and wait for things to blow over.

On Sunday 2 October, Marcel landed in Orly. All he could say was: 'I want La Motta. No one else. In the Polo Grounds, in Madison Square Garden, in a barn if he wants, without any witnesses except a judge and journalists. It's got nothing to do with money.' He had tears in his eyes.

It was a year and a day since his triumphant return after defeating Tony Zale.

15

Take-Off

Edith came on at the Versailles at 10.00 p.m. and 1.00 a.m. every evening. Overnight, the club was making more than it had for over fifteen years. A bottle of champagne (from France) cost $16 and a sirloin steak $6.50. Edith was breaking all the records. There seemed to be no limit to people's praise: 'She's better than ever', 'She's greater than . . . Sarah Bernhardt', 'She's amazing, she's absolutely enchanting', 'She's taken New York by storm.'

She was inundated with offers. She was invited to Hollywood, to Chicago; they wanted her in San Francisco; from there she could go to Florida, or Mexico . . .

But away from the flattery, promises and projects, Edith felt very alone. Every evening when she went back to the flat, arm in arm with Genevieve, all she could talk about was Marcel in Casablanca. She was dying of frustration. It hurt not to be able to see and hear him, not to be able to speak or write to him. She cursed fate, cursed his absence (which was already weighing on her) and cursed wretched La Motta for backing down. She told Genevieve in a flat voice: 'He's a bastard. But we'll have our revenge, and how!'

She wanted the fight to take place the next day, immediately, now. She went to bed earlier than usual. She would open a book but the words danced in front of her eyes. She couldn't read. She tried to imagine him . . .

Marcel had taken up tennis again. He played for two hours every morning. He was philosophical about his bad luck. He kept his mind off things by devoting himself wholeheartedly to his family. He played pétanque with his brother Armand and Narcisse Lopez. He started his training again from square one. He sparred with his nephew René. One of his ambitions was to make René a champion. He was very strict with him, trying to inculcate a boxer's self-discipline. He took him to see Honoré Pratesi defeat Bobhot. When he wasn't in the ASPTT gym or in his bar, he was up in the hills of Anfa inspecting the villa that was being built for him.

Marinette, his wife, had never known him to take such pleasure in home life. They would chat for ages after the children had gone to bed. Marcel was obsessed by his children's future. He wanted to send Marcel Junior to the Institut Jeanne-d'Arc, run by nuns, and then to high school. His everyday existence was uneventful, except that he was burning with impatience to cross swords with La Motta. He knew that Burston was doing the impossible in New York, that people were running around, holding talks, negotiating. He was waiting for some sign from Longman. He even took the initiative. For the first time ever, he phoned Paris himself. Longman was staggered. He always had no end of trouble getting hold of Marcel. He often had to fly out to Casablanca himself, and once he had to hire a donkey to seek him out in the interior!

Then came the news Marcel was waiting for. La Motta's agreement was imminent. Marcel had to get ready to return to Paris. The day before his departure, after a last family meal at the Sidi Marouf farm, to please Marinette, Marcel suggested they go out to the Don Quichotte, a big night-club in Casablanca. There was no holding him back. He led Marinette out onto the dance floor. She liked dancing with him. He had taught her the tango, the samba and the bolero.

The next day, 23 October, Marcel flew to Paris. He didn't want Marinette to accompany him to the airport. While she was packing his case, he told her: 'This'll be my last fight. Don't listen to the radio. I'll win.'

In Paris, Marcel stayed at Jo Longman's house in the rue de Provence. He was a bundle of nerves. A first cable announced that La Motta was on the point of signing. Burston asked Jo and Marcel to stand by. There would be another message soon . . . A few hours went by. Burston was playing a tight game in New York. The organisers had had difficulty finding room in Madison Square Garden's heavily booked programme. La Motta had seemed to agree to 2 December. Now, all of a sudden, he was pulling out to get publicity. And, to top it all, he was demanding an extra $1,000 for the television rights.

La Motta went too far. They ended up threatening to relegate him to the list of 'ill or unavailable boxers'. There was even talk of leaving the title vacant should Jake continue to be awkward. Jake finally agreed to sign. Burston immediately alerted his friends in Paris. His telegram said that La Motta had given him every assurance and that the world championship would take place on the date planned.

Marcel jumped for joy in the flat. 'Wonderful!' he shouted. He wanted to leave for America immediately.

Longman calmed him down. 'Marcel, don't forget your exhibition bout at Troyes.'

'I haven't forgotten,' replied Marcel, 'but nor have I forgotten that I've got to be on the spot at least twenty-five days before the fight.'

Why did she have to phone him then?

She wasn't OK. She was in a terrible mood. She was having rows with everyone in New York. She could

211

do nothing but find fault with her friends. She and Genevieve had a scene over nothing. They went to see a ballet arranged and danced by Roland Petit. At supper Genevieve had felt she ought to pay him a compliment. She said she had particularly liked a *pas de deux*. Roland Petit had nodded his assent. Edith had sniggered. 'Poor Genevieve,' she had giggled, 'it was the only movement Roland had nothing to do with.'

They had walked back to the apartment. Edith had launched into Genevieve again as if she had taken a sudden dislike to her. 'What a clanger you dropped, my dear.'

Genevieve let her finish before striking back somewhat haughtily: 'Frankly, Edith, you overdo things.'

Edith was cutting. 'And who on earth do you take yourself for, Madame Lévitan?'

Genevieve was in the process of packing her bags when Edith appeared in her room. 'Forgive me, I didn't mean it. I can't stop myself.' Then she burst into tears. 'Why must I destroy everything?' Genevieve held her in her arms.

She heard his fluty laugh on the phone. He was euphoric. They were on opposite sides of the Atlantic. They were half happy, half sad. He told her everything.

She pressed him: 'So, you'll be here soon?'

'Yes, I'm going to arrange it. We'll take the boat as soon as possible.'

'The boat? You must be joking. Take the plane, Marcel, I need you.'

So he promised her to be there even sooner. The next day, an article signed by Marcel Cerdan and written by René Dunan made the *France-Soir* headlines:

'Once, through stupidity, a silly accident, La Motta

212

got me. Once is enough . . . It won't happen a second time. I must beat La Motta, and beat him I shall. I will be at my peak on 2 December. Believe me, I shall return to France with the world middleweight crown firmly on my head. Unfortunately, the Evans Hotel, where I usually train, is now closed. It is too late in the season. But Jo Longman is negotiating with several training camps. We shall set ourselves up in the middle of the countryside, most probably about sixty miles away at Greenwood Lake. Willy Ketchum who trained me for the match that didn't take place in September will be back with us.'

Marcel, Wednesday, 26 September 1949, Troyes
Marcel resigned himself to the exhibition bout. It was organised by Charly Mittel, one of the founders of the Club des Cinq, and a close friend of Jo Longman's since the African campaign with the 2nd Armoured Division. Mittel ran an off-the-peg clothing shop in the rue du Commerce, in the fifteenth arrondissement in Paris. His made-to-measure motto was: '*Honni soit qui mal se vêt*' (He who dresses badly shall be held in contempt). He promised that 'Anyone referred by Marcel Cerdan shall be entitled to a reduction.'

He had organised the fight in the municipal circus to celebrate the opening of a new branch in Troyes. To please Charly and for old times' sake, Marcel graciously agreed to attend all the receptions given in their honour. A reporter on *France-Dimanche*, Jacques Chapus, kept a careful note of his busy timetable.

Marcel arrived in Troyes around ten in the morning. Wherever he went – to the newspaper, the *Petit Troyen*, to see the mayor at the town hall, and in the headquarters of the local club, *L'Energie troyenne* – he had a smile on his face. It was one of his open, slightly teasing smiles.

213

He was happy, calm and very much in control. He was inundated with questions. He told everyone: 'I'm leaving tomorrow for New York. It's the most important trip of my career. I want to become world champion again. Firstly, for myself, for my own personal pride, but also for all of you who've put your faith in me.'

There was applause. He had lunch in the restaurant *La Bourgogne*, then went on to Charly Mittel's shop, *A la ville de Paris*. There was a scrum. He signed autograph after autograph. He gave photos of himself to everyone, children, women, sportsmen and would-be sportsmen, always adding a kind word.

Longman shouted at him: 'Stop, take a break.'

Marcel waved him away. 'It's OK, Jo, I'm not tired.'

The municipal circus was crowded that evening. The programme had already started when Marcel arrived. He drank in the atmosphere. He gave his bag to Longman. 'Take it to the cloakroom. I want to see the boxing.' He mixed with the other spectators and got caught up in all the amateur fights which opened the show. Then came his turn to get ready. He joined Jo in the changing-rooms. It was a circus dressing-room, covered with photos of film stars.

Jo and Paul Genser watched him dress. Marcel got onto the scales. He weighed 162 pounds.

'If you only knew, Jo,' said Marcel, 'how well I feel.'

'Too well, I fear,' replied Longman. 'You are too fit, too light, for someone who still has six weeks to go to the world championship.'

'It's not a serious problem,' said Marcel. 'We'll lounge around in New York for four or five days. You'll see, I'll put on weight again.'

'Won't you stay on in Paris for a few more days?' Longman was trying to get Marcel to change his mind. 'You know,' he went on, 'we really could leave next

Tuesday. We'd be able to go to the Palais des Sports on Monday evening. That would give us time to get ready for the journey.'

'No, no, Jo,' said Cerdan excitedly, 'we can't wait. Friday's a good day to arrive in New York. We'll make all the weekend newspapers.'

Longman was tired of arguing and gave up. He made a joke of it: 'My word, Marcel, so you're the businessman now, are you?'

Marcel smeared his face with vaseline, put on his purple American Everdast shorts, threw his robe over his shoulders and went back to mingle with the crowd in the hall for a few more minutes while he waited his turn. He watched the ring, isolated like a brilliant raft in a sea of shadows. Then he was called. At 10.15 the Master of Ceremonies Tafanelli announced him to the public.

Tafanelli cleared his throat and said in a voice everyone could hear: 'Every time I have the honour of introducing Cerdan, I try to find a new way of doing it. But whatever I come up with is a waste of time.' Tafanelli waited for silence, and with a theatrical gesture, held his arm out to the champion's corner, raised his voice and, emphasising each syllable, he announced: 'Here is Mar-cel Cer-dan!'

Marcel sprang over the ropes. He was received with noisy applause. Valère Benedetto, a young welterweight from Arles, had been chosen to fight him. He was very intimidated and drew near to Cerdan to whisper in his ear: 'How do we play it?'

Marcel reassured him: 'Don't worry. Hit me and I'll try and hit you.'

But Benedetto had learned his lesson by heart. He had been told that in the last seconds of each of the three rounds, Longman would blow on a whistle. At this point the boxers would face each other and do a few staged sequences. People loved these rhythmic exercises.

215

The three rounds went very quickly. Marcel gave the impression of great strength and lightness. He ended with a left hook – the left which had let him down when he fought La Motta and which he had since worked on. The audience was delighted and cheered wildly. Marcel thanked them and Tafanelli took up the microphone again. He had one last announcement to make: 'It gives me great pleasure to be able to say that Marcel is handing his fee over to local charities.'

Marcel was in no hurry to leave. He savoured his triumph like a beginner. Paul, Jo and Marcel didn't leave the dinner table until two in the morning, when they decided to go back to Paris.

Andy Dickson, then a junior reporter on the *Parisien Libéré*, remembers that day:

'I was the only Parisian sports reporter that evening at the Troyes circus. Marcel, who had boxed wearing a leather helmet, made a strong impression on me. He had literally knocked the wind out of his opponent, who had a reputation for being very fast. I was preparing to go back to the hotel, thinking I would take the first train in the morning, when I met Jo Longman. He immediately suggested that I go back with them.

'People in the boxing world were very friendly towards me, not because I was a young journalist but because I was the son of Jeff Dickson. My father had been a great figure in the Vélodrome d'Hiver before the war. He was dead – he had been a pilot and was killed in 1943.

'There was room for one more in the car. We had to squeeze up. Paul Genser sat to the right of the driver. I was directly behind him. Marcel was in the middle and Jo Longman on the other side. It was

216

very late when we set off. Marcel fell asleep straight away, or almost straight away. When we came to a bend his head would fall onto Jo's shoulder or mine. I didn't dare move. I was too star-struck. Paul, Jo and I talked incessantly. Marcel was going to beat La Motta. It was obvious to all three of us. He had all the trumps in his hand. We competed with each other to list attributes that would win him the match. It was a foregone conclusion. We were driving quite fast.

'Marcel woke up briefly between Nogent-sur-Seine and Provins, listened to us for a few seconds as we discussed his forthcoming world championship and put in his word: "Listen, leave me in peace, I'm going to beat this La Motta, but let me get some sleep." I can still hear him saying it. We arrived in Paris at day break. They left me at the metro stop on the Quai de Bercy. I was living with my mother in Sartrouville.'

By lunchtime, the comfortable flat shared by Jo Longman and Jacqueline on the fifth floor in the rue de Provence looked like the Marx Brothers' cabin in *A Night at the Opera*. Jo and Marcel were throwing things into their cases. It was a scene of busy but lighthearted chaos. The atmosphere was relaxed. Marcel kept playing his favourite record: 'Riders in the Sky'.

They grabbed a quick snack. Jacques Meyran, a variety artiste and one of Edith Piaf's confidants, had offered to take them to Orly. Marcel had on a grey tweed overcoat over the blue suit he wore for luck whenever he flew. Carrying his heavy suitcase on his shoulder he rushed down the stairs, followed by Jo. He sat in the front of the royal blue Pontiac Jacques Meyran was driving. Jo and Paul Genser sat in the back.

Meyran was about to start when Longman, who had

been checking to see they had everything, cried out: 'Damn! We've left the passports behind. I'll go back and get them. Wait for me, Meyran, I won't be a minute . . .'

Finally they left. It was late. Longman was jumping up and down. The plane would be taking off in two hours' time. And then Marcel had an idea. 'Let's go and say goodbye to the girls.'

Jo didn't agree: 'We haven't got time.'

Marcel stuck to his guns. 'We can't leave without saying goodbye.'

The Pontiac drew up front of the Ambassade de l'Opéra in the rue Sainte-Anne. The little restaurant was still empty. Marcel went behind the bar and embraced Mado Fondo, Irene de Trébert, his buddy Jacquot the barman, and Denis, known as Néné, Mado's brother, who was devoted to him.

An edgy Longman appeared on the threshold. 'Hurry up, we'll miss the plane . . .'

It was eight o'clock according to the big clock in Orly airport. All of a sudden, the word spread through the hall to the ticket counters: 'Cerdan's here!' The photographers were waiting for him and jostled with each other. Ten microphones were held out at the same time. Marcel faced up to the flash like an old hand, spoke into one microphone and leaned comfortably over another, repeating the same thing: 'I shall be bringing back the crown I lost. I'm going to fight like a lion. I shall be starting my training in three days' time. I can't wait to get back to New York and the Madison Square Garden ring. If I could have left earlier I would have. I had to lean on Air France to get a priority seat on the Paris–New York flight.'

The whole of France was listening. For millions, Cerdan's departure overshadowed the fact that after three weeks of unhappy experiments, the French President,

Vincent Auriol, had finally found a new government leader in Georges Bidault.

Marcel added: 'I shall use every ounce of strength I have to regain the title which I was stupid enough to lose. At the age of thirty-three, with a hundred and sixteen fights behind me . . .'

'Wrong, Marcel. A hundred and nineteen,' someone whispered.

'A hundred and nineteen then,' he smiled. 'It makes no difference. I feel nowhere near worn out or too old.' Marcel was very articulate that evening. 'When the time comes, I'll know how to stop without being pushed.'

Longman was more down to earth. 'We're slipping away like thieves,' he apologised. He raised his eyes. 'But we simply can't keep him here a minute longer. If he had taken my advice we would have spent the whole week in Paris. We would have flown on Tuesday. It would have been much simpler. But no, we had to go now. I have the feeling we've forgotten half the things we need.'

Marcel signed his autograph on cards, handkerchiefs, metro tickets. A taxi driver brought him a boxing glove to sign. He thanked him, crying like a child. A voice was heard: 'Are you wearing your blue suit, Marcel?'

He nodded and gripped the lapel of his jacket. All his fans knew how superstitious he was. Strangely enough, no one paid any attention to the predictions made by the palmist Arista. He had asked to see the champion. The meeting had taken place at Paul's in the rue d'Orsel. Arista had looked at Cerdan's hand and warned him in an earnest voice: 'You fly too often. Watch out. . . .'

'I can't help it.' Marcel had replied. 'I have to travel.'

Later on, Arista had stretched his 'professional conscience' to ask for a copy of Marcel Cerdan's birth certificate from the town hall in Sidi Bel Abbes. He had then drawn up his horoscope. There it was for all to read: 'Try not to travel by air, especially on Fridays.'

Now Marcel was being pressed into having his photograph taken with Ginette Neveu. He grimaced. It was not that he had the slightest grudge against the great violinist who had just given a triumphant recital at Pleyel of the thirty-two Chacone variations by Bach; but Cerdan was wary of posed photos which could always be used against you. It had happened before . . .

Nevertheless, he let himself be persuaded. 'For posterity', he gazed respectfully at the Stradivarius which Ginette Neveu had taken out of its case, and he now gripped in his thick fingers. She played a few chords for the photographers. The reporters were happy. Marcel then took his friends off for a last drink. Maurice, the barman at Orly, knew what he liked. He had already chilled, without freezing it, a bottle of extra dry champagne which Marcel drank slowly, as befits a connoisseur. Jo Longman, visibly preoccupied, forgot to drink.

Marcel kidded him. He remarked to Maurice that Jo was like a wet blanket that evening. Luckily, his friend Paul was at his side, full of beans, laughing and humming a tune, the life and soul of the party.

And now the time had come to say goodbye. Marcel grabbed the hands held out to him, shouted a joyous 'See you soon' to Maurice and went off to the newspaper kiosk. He gave the saleswoman fifty francs and hurried off.

'Your change, Monsieur Cerdan,' she cried.

He turned round and replied with a smile: 'Give it to me next time.'

It was a cold clear night. The passengers pulled up the collars of their coats as they climbed the gangway in single file. The steward said there were thirty-seven of them.

Three passengers had had to give up their seats at

the last minute: Mr and Mrs Newton, a recently married American couple and Mme Erdmann, a Parisienne. Marcel, Jo and Paul were given their seats. The three of them were ushered down the gangway by Monsieur Guirant, the manager of Orly airport, who had been a friend of Cerdan's for ten years.

They took their seats on the plane as it stood waiting in front of the airport.

Marcel and Jo sat side by side, in the middle of the plane, Marcel next to the porthole. Paul was behind Jo. Opposite them, on the other side of the aisle was Bertrand Boutet de Monvel, who painted American high society, fine horsemen and polo players. He designed the posters for Ingrid Bergman's films. Americans paid a high price for his portraits. His painting of Jeanne d'Arc had won him international renown.

Seated in front of Marcel was Mme Jenny Brandière, aged forty, and her daughter, Françoise, who was twenty-one. Four months earlier, Mme Brandière had rushed to her daughter's bedside, after she had been seriously injured in a car crash. Françoise was considered beyond hope. She had recovered, and mother and daughter were off again to Cuba where they lived.

In the first row was Mrs Hennessy, a face well known to Air France. She had arrived late at Orly. They had tried to turn her away. She had thrown a tantrum and insisted. She got her way in the end.

Sitting at the very back were five Basques flushed with excitement. Three of them were from the village of Aldudes. They were shepherds. They were called Siquil-bide, Chourrout, Aduritz, Etchepare and Arambel. They had never been further than Bayonne. The day before they had climbed the Eiffel Tower. They were going to the American West to make their fortunes, as the pioneers had done before them.

221

There was also Guy Jasmin, a journalist on *Canada Montréal* and his wife; Mr Kay Kamen, director of the Walt Disney Studios; and Jean Paul, Ginette Neveu's brother, who sat next to his sister. From the departure area you could see Marcel's familiar wave at the porthole.

At 9.06 p.m. the Constellation FBA-ZN, equipped with four 2,500 horse power Wright cyclone engines, took off amidst a deafening roar. There were forty-eight people on board, including extra cabin staff, who had been brought in especially. The plane was full in terms of total weight, passengers and freight. There was nothing unusual about the take-off. Planes took off all the time for New York. It was no more significant than the departure of a train for Marseilles. Forty planes crossed the Atlantic every day. Since 1 July 1946 Air France had carried 52,000 passengers on 1,972 crossings, each taking seventeen hours. There had never been an accident. The Constellation was due to make two stops en route: the Azores and Gander (Newfoundland), before reaching New York, at 9.30 a.m.

The captain of the FBA-ZN was Jean de la Noue. A former sailor, he had been a pilot since 1935 and had trained numerous commercial pilots. He had been flying the North Atlantic route for the past two years. He had crossed the ocean eighty-eight times and had accumulated nearly seven thousand hours of flying time. He was thirty-seven and had three children.

At 11.00 p.m. Paris time, the Constellation gave its first position: west of Rochefort. The second position was communicated at midnight: A.O.K. Third position, 1.00 a.m.: A.O.K. 200 miles west of Portugal. Fourth position, 2.00 a.m.: A.O.K. The plane indicated that it would be arriving in the Azores at 3.50.

3.50: The plane asked for landing instructions from the control tower on Santa Maria, the most southerly of the islands in the archipelago. It was midnight in the Azores. It was clear; visibility: twelve miles. The island of Sao Miguel and the Rodonta peak (3,500 feet) were on the right.

The control tower replied that everything was ready for landing and that the plane should come in from the south. It was to reduce speed to 260 miles per hour.

The FBA-ZN replied: 'OK. We're at 3,000 feet. We land in five minutes.'

Epilogue

'Si un jour la vie t'arrache à moi . . .'
(If life should tear you from me one day)

Edith, 28 October, 136 East, Lexington 67th Street, New York, 1.30 p.m.

Edith screamed and collapsed. Loulou Barrier's silence had told her everything. The others – Chauvigny, Bonel, Burston, Genevieve Lévitan – were all impotent and helpless, caught up in their own sorrow. They were all mourning Marcel in their different ways. It was Barrier again who tried to pick Edith up. Everyone in the apartment was overwhelmed. Instinctively, they all kept an eye on the windows, watching Edith closely. Poor little woman. Her crying had given way to moans. She threw herself against the base of a lampstand near the sofa. Genevieve put an arm round her shoulders and guided her gently towards her room. She offered her a glass of water but Edith shook her head. She crumpled up on the end of the bed like a rag doll or an abandoned puppy.

Lew Burston had been fully aware of the tragedy for a while. The phone had rung in the middle of the night in his Manhattan apartment. It was a reporter. Lew had been fast asleep and had been surprised that anyone should disturb him so late. He had been about to hang up on

224

this intruder when he heard him ask in a breathless voice: 'Lew, have you heard the news?'

Burston couldn't sleep for the rest of the night. When he got up at 7.00 a.m., his brown hair had turned grey, as it remains to this day. Burston felt he had a mission: to protect Edith in her suffering and to ensure respect for Marcel's death . . .

There were about ten press photographers and reporters in the stairway still battling for a comment or photo. They all used different lines to try and get a foot in the door. One of them cried out that there was still hope. Burston pushed him aside: 'Please leave us alone.' He called a doctor. The doctor had to push his way through the crowd outside before he could get to the apartment. He made Edith take a tranquilliser.

Barrier spoke to Clifford Fischer on the phone: 'No, Clifford, forget it, it's impossible.' Fischer wanted to know what sort of a state Edith was in.

'She's lost everything, Clifford, everything.' Barrier asked Fischer to warn Provys, the manager of the Versailles, that Edith wouldn't be singing that evening.

Since he had given her a second chance after the Playhouse two years ago, Provys had always gone out of his way to show Edith the kind of consideration she appreciated. It was typical that he should now come over with Fischer, bearing a flask of soup. It was his way of warming up his little French woman's body and soul. Piaf had got into the habit of drinking his bouillon every evening before going on stage at the Versailles.

Provys opened her bedroom door carefully. He leaned over Edith and spoke a few tender words. He talked to her about Marcel whom he knew well. 'He was my friend as well, you know.'

She lifted up her head and thanked him with her swollen eyes.

225

'It's terrible, terrible for everyone,' Provys went on. 'Don't worry about this evening, I'll sort something out.'

She came down to earth. 'There's nothing to sort out. I shall sing . . . for him.'

She had always had an incredible instinct for survival. She agreed to see a reporter-photographer from the *Daily News*, Tom Baffer. But no one else. She knew she had to meet her responsibilities towards the public. She also knew that the whole of New York knew. She had to face the city as well.

She posed for two photos. The reporter then plucked up his courage and asked her a question. 'And now, Madame, what are your plans?'

Edith burst into tears. 'Oh, Marcel!'

Lew Burston signalled to the photographer to withdraw.

Edith collapsed into the arms of Genevieve, who proceeded to dress her for the show.

She usually left the apartment around 9.00 p.m. and arrived at the Versailles half an hour before she went on. It was 7.30 p.m. that evening when she went down into Lexington Avenue. Together with Mrs Lew Burston, Genevieve and Loulou Barrier, she let herself be taken to the first church they saw. It was a block away in St Vincent Ferrier Street, on the corner of 66th Street.

She wanted to persuade herself that Marcel was still alive. She lit a candle.

There were more photographers when they came out. Loulou kept them away and hid Edith behind his wool coat.

There was a feverish atmosphere outside the main entrance to the Versailles. Everyone was caught up in the drama. People wanted to catch a glimpse of Edith as she went in through the main entrance. And the tables next to the stage were going for $100 each.

In Madison Square Garden where a big basketball evening was in progress, the announcer's voice could be heard above the excitement. 'Marcel Cerdan was killed in the Paris–New York plane crash.' The excitement faded. There was a short silence, a few murmurs and then the crowd sang the American anthem. A few people could be heard singing 'La Marseillaise'.

At 10.10 Marc Bonel clung to his accordion in the Versailles, his eyes full of tears. He had just started to play 'La vie en rose'.

Edith embraced both him and Robert Chauvigny, her pianist. She had calmed down. She had tried to put some life into her chalk-like face.

The audience gave her a frenetic welcome with an enormous round of applause. She stopped them.

'This evening I shall be singing for Marcel Cerdan.'

She was supposed to sing eight songs. She sang only four.

She started to sing "Hymne à l'amour':

> 'Le ciel bleu sur nous peut s'effondrer
> Et la terre peut bien s'écrouler'
> (The blue sky can collapse on us/And the earth can give way)

All you could hear now was the music. Eventually, a few more words came out:

> 'Si un jour, la vie t'arrache à moi
> Si tu meurs, que tu sois loin de moi . . .'
> (If one day life tears you from me/If you should die, and be far from me . . .).

She fainted. The curtain came down, shrouding her.

New York le 3. 11. 49

Félix

Je ne peux pas retrouver mon calme, je
ne peux que pleurer toute la journée.
C'est affreux Félix affreux.' Ta femme
doit être maintenant près de toi, garde la
bien contre toi, ne vous séparez plus
jamais, c'est trop terrible quand on réalise
ce que l'on a perdu. Je ne m'en remettrai
jamais. Je voudrais tant mourir, pourquoi
Dieu n'a t'il pas pitié de moi, je veux
être là ou il est je le veux! je sais combien
tu l'aimais et tu sais a quel point
je l'adorais. Pense que nous devrions être
si heureux et que je suis si atrocement
malheureuse. Écris moi, tes lettres me font
tant de bien et j'en ai tant besoin Merci de
m'avoir laissé ta Geneviève, maintenant qu'elle
est partie mon chagrin est encore plus grand.
Nous étions parties si pleines de joies
oh Félix c'est trop cruel.
Je ne sais plus quoi t'écrire, mon
esprit est vide de tout.
Je t'embrasse de tout mon chagrin
Edith

228

Letter to Felix Lévitan, written four days after the event

New York 3.11.49

Dear Felix,

I'm in such a state, all I can do is cry. It's terrible, Felix, terrible. Your wife must be with you by now, keep her close, *never* leave each other again; it's too awful when you realise what you've lost. I'll never get over it. All I want to do is die. Why can't God have pity on me? I want to be where he is! I know how much you loved him and you know how I adored him. To think how happy we should have been and how miserable I am now. Write – your letters do me so much good. I need to hear from you. Thank you for lending me your Genevieve. Now she has gone, my burden of sorrow is even greater. We were so cheerful when we left Paris. O Felix, it's too cruel!

I don't know what else to write, my heart is empty.

I embrace you in the depths of my sorrow.

Edith

New York le 3/III 49

Ma Geneviève

Quel vide, quel grand vide ! Oh je t'en suplie, fais quelque chose pour moi, prie toi qui ne l'a jamais fait prie pour que j'aille le rejoindre, il m'est impossible de vivre sans lui c'est pire chaque jour, c'est affreux comme tu dois être heureuse et comme je t'envie. Ecris moi souvent, il le faut ! As tu vu ton docteur qui s'occupe des sciences occultes ? J'en ai vraiment besoin, je veux être en contact avec Marcel, je veux savoir s'il est quelque part a m'attendre ! Vois tu ce qu'il y a de terrible c'est que je l'aime encore plus fort qu'avant, on dirait que c'est lui même qui rentre encore plus dans moi, je suis imprégnée de lui partout, jamais jamais je ne l'ai autant aimé ! Geneviève je ne peux plus t'écrire je ne vois plus clair et j'ai tant envie de sangloter.

Je t'embrasse ma grande amie
Edith

Letter to Genevieve Lévitan, the same day

New York 3.11.49

My dear Genevieve,
What emptiness. What great emptiness! I beg you, do
something for me. You, who've never prayed, pray for
me to be reunited with him. I can't live without him. It
gets worse every day, it's terrible. You must be so happy.
How I envy you. You must write to me often! Have you
seen your doctor who is interested in the occult? I really
need help. I want to make contact with Marcel, I want to
know if he's waiting for me somewhere! The awful thing
is that I love him more than before, he seems to be
working his way deeper and deeper inside me, he fills
my every pore. I love him more than ever. I can't write
any more, Genevieve, everything is hazy and all I want
to do is cry.

I embrace you, my dear friend.

Edith

Edith Piaf lived another fourteen years,
but her life was never complete again.

Acknowledgements

The authors would like to thank all those whose personal accounts contributed to this book. Particular thanks go to: Genevieve and Felix Lévitan, Irene de Trébert, Marc and Danièle Bonel, Loulou Barrier, Michel Emer, Ginette Richer (Ginou), Jean-Louis Jaubert, The Compagnons de la Chanson, Jean Walczak. The authors would also like to express their gratitude to: Max Corre, Georges Cravenne, Robert Bré, Andy Dickson, Charles Dumont, Mado Fondo, Dominique France, Maurice Fonsèque, Hubert Lancelot and Louis Sapin; Bert Sugar (chief editor, *Ring Magazine*, New York), John Condon (Manager, Madison Square Garden), Harold Weston (Boxing Manager, Madison Square Garden), Eleanor Brown (former telephone operator, Evans Hotel, Loch Sheldrake, N.Y.), Gwen Evans (Loch Sheldrake, N.Y.), Andrew Neiderman (writer, Fallsburg, Sullivan County, N.Y.); and Mme Belcourt and Philippe Dumont, currently resident in the houses inhabited by Piaf and Cerdan, 7 rue Leconte de Lisle (Paris 16) and 5 rue Gambetta in the Bois de Boulogne.

Research was carried out with the assistance of the Arts Research Center, Lincoln Center, New York, The New York Public Library, The Catskills Museum, Hurleyville (Sullivan County, N.Y.). Archives were made available by Le Sportsman and La Galcante, Paris. Picture research was conducted by François Gragnon. Assistance with documentation was provided by Hubert d'Havrincourt. Research was undertaken in France and the United States by Dominique Grimault, Patrick Mahé and Martine Audouin.

Bibliography

Piaf, Simone Berteaut, Robert Laffont (English version: W. H. Allen)
Histoire de Piaf, Monique Lange, Ramsay (English version: W. H. Allen)
La Môme Piaf, Auguste Le Breton, Hachette
Piaf, Ma Soeur, Denise Gassion, Guy Authier
Edith Piaf, Jean Noli, Presse Pocket

Cerdan, Marinette Cerdan and René Cerdan, Solar, Sports 2000
Ma Vie, Mes Combats, Marcel Cerdan, *France-Soir*
Cerdan, La Vérité, Lucien Roupp, Presses de la Cité
Dix Ans avec Marcel Cerdan, Lucien Roupp, Ed. du Scorpion
Les Cerdan, Roland Passevant, Dargaud
L'Homme aux Mains d'Argile, Marcel Rivet, Ed. de Flore

Raging Bull, Jake La Motta, Bantam Books
Chaud Business, Charley Michaelis, Solar, Sports 2000
Mon Après-Guerre, F. Brigneau, Ed. du Clan
Le Roman de la IVe République, Gilbert Guilleminault, Denoël

In the course of their research, the authors consulted the following newspapers and magazines: *Paris-Match, Le Parisien Libéré, France-Soir, Paris-Presse, Le Figaro, Ce Soir,*

Libération, Samedi Soir, France-Dimanche, Radar, Ambiance, Flash, Radio 47, Point de Vue, Sports Sélection, Sport Digest, Miroir Sprint, But and Club, New York Daily News, New York Herald Tribune, New York Times, New York Journal American, New York Post, New York Daily Mirror, New York World Telegram, The Sunday Republican (Loch Sheldrake, Monticello), and *The Sullivan Democrat* (Loch Sheldrake, Monticello).